Enriched Marketing

Empower your brand with the perfect client

NATALIE DENT

**SUSS
INKED
PUBLISHING**

First published in 2024 by Suss Inked
Paperback ISBN-13: 978-1-7392829-1-2
eBook ISBN-13: 978-1-7392829-2-9

Edited by Harriet Power
Cover design by CanalPath
Illustrations by CanalPath

You can achieve great things, but the work needs to ultimately come from you.

For Rob,
who always lifts me up to see
beyond the clouds.

THIS BOOK IS DESIGNED TO LET THE PIECES
FALL INTO PLACE AS YOU GO

Contents

SECTION 3
DEFINING YOUR BRAND'S PERSONALITY

SECTION 4
SETTING UP YOUR ENRICHED MARKETING STRATEGY

SECTION 5
FINDING BOTH MONEY AND JOY IN YOUR BUSINESS

A Short Intro

Enriched marketing pays homage to all the incredible psychologists, philosophers, marketers, and trillion-dollar brands that have left their marks on the world.

Eugene Schwartz was one of the most influential copywriters of all time. Carl Jung condensed our inherent human psychologies into a simple framework that's impacted the advertising industry for generations. Dan Kennedy championed entrepreneurs with the power of inbound marketing, while Steve Jobs showed us the value of selling ideas over admin, and Disney coined the phrase, 'Imagineering'.

My shelves are sagging with the immense value held in the books I've read about harnessing human stories, but there's always been something missing.

How does all this knowledge fit together in a simple way that lets the humble entrepreneur with a big dream build a highly profitable business?

For the last 20+ years, I've dedicated my life's work to answering this question. Enriched Marketing as a concept is designed to weave the golden threads together in a logical format that makes building powerful brand stories intuitive, even if you are just one person without a significant marketing budget.

My goal is to create a world where the secrets of sales communication are accessible and easy to use for everyone who wants to discover them.

I want to consolidate everything I've learned by reading obsessively, working with successful brands, and observing the foundations of human nature, into a simple yet powerful strategy for anyone who looks to make a lasting impact on their audience.

This book is your ticket to the brand you hope to build. If you have any questions, feel free to reach out.

It's easy to think that being rich and successful is just for big brands with huge budgets, but this isn't the case at all. Being rich and successful is for people with the right story. Anyone can have a powerful brand story because stories are made from words, and everyone has access to words.

Best,

Natalie

A NOTE ON 'NORMAL MARKETING' – AND WHY IT NEARLY ALWAYS FALLS FLAT

I F you're reading this book, chances are you've worked with more than a few bad clients over the years. You know the sort. They suck your joy and leave you feeling a little frazzled.

Like all business owners, you probably started out with excellent intent. You have valuable ideas for doing something you love, and you've done everything the marketing experts have advised, so why isn't it working?

Why are you still explaining what you do to the same old faces, chasing the same types of disinterested clients, and working far too hard for far too little reward?

Sometimes, a few years will go by before you take an honest look at your business for what it is. When you do, you'll likely find the business dream you once had is still struggling along in the background, jaded by all the wrong types of clients *who just don't get it*.

This can be so disheartening, especially if everything should be working, but just isn't for no obvious reason.

Far from the anticipated Insta-worthy, superb work-life balance of lattes and long walks on the beach, a business caught in a bad-client trap is a continuous juggling act. You've got too many low-ball prospects that keep you running around doing a lot of work, but still don't experience the joy or the free time that owning your own business promised to deliver when you reached up and took your business dreams into your hands.

I used to run my business like this too, before my dream clients – many of whom now effortlessly generate over seven figures a year – taught me a simple truth.

Business owners attract the types of clients they design into their own businesses, whether they mean to or not.

REACTIVE BUSINESSES STRUGGLE TO THRIVE, BUT DON'T ALWAYS KNOW WHY.

Business owners can be reactive to a fault. People say, 'Are you good at that, can you help?'

Then you just say yes and figure it out as you go, until somebody else asks for something slightly different, and you say yes again. Perhaps a mediocre client recommends you to a friend or you see an unexpected opportunity somewhere. You say yes again, and again.

Entrepreneurs will frequently do anything offered just to collect some revenue or build a fledgling client base. This is a big part of having the grit to start something from nothing, which not everyone can do, but it's also the start of so many problems to come for the average start-up business.

With this 'always-say-yes' approach, the business grows day

by day, with one less-than-ideal job after the next far-from-favourable project.

Eventually, after a few years of learning on the job, fighting fires and chasing your tail, you'll look back to find you've built up quality skills and plenty of experience doing all *sorts* of different types of things for your variety of clients, but your business is somehow filled with an endless flow of people who fail to ignite your full potential.

Bad clients, who still don't know what you're worth!

If you're anything like the average entrepreneur, your definition of what the dream client actually looks like is muddled and murky, and you're not quite sure what you're trying to achieve.

People in business habitually do what works, and many things *do* work, but they don't always know why it works, which makes every new solution a risky guess that may or may not get you to the right place tomorrow. These risks drive further reactive experiments, which cause an unfavourable cycle of trial and error that can win or lose on any given day.

A 'normal marketing' reaction is nearly always to redefine your unique selling points (USPs), research better content marketing providers, spend more time on social media, crank up your efforts in local networking groups, and up your advertising.

If you keep punting the idea, someone will buy into it eventually, because you *know* you have something good, and you genuinely believe there's a buyer for everything.

Somewhere in the chaos of trying to get yourself out of the bad-client loop, deadlines take over. All those to-do lists continue to grow faster than your business, and the cycle of 'win or lose today' eventually cracks.

So you beat on, doing whatever you can do for whoever wants you to do it, until you crash, burn, or quit!

Bad clients can all too easily let you feel like you're just doing the work because you *have to* do it; because you need to take on every job that comes your way just to stay afloat.

This 'always-say-yes' syndrome is a guaranteed way to design a business that sets you up to fail. It creates upside-down thinking that magics the wrong types of people into your business ecosystem, and makes them nearly impossible to remove!

The end result of trying to market a reactive business that develops as you go is a collection of fundamentally flawed clients who inherently work against you, not for you, even when they pay on time and show up with a friendly face.

These are the people who use your resources without adding much value to your wider business objectives. They soak up your time, whitewash your energy, and leave you wondering if running the business of your dreams will *ever* be worth it!

When you run a business like this – using 'always-say-yes' tactics that keep you chasing scarce demand – marketing can start to feel all over the place.

New trends on social media seem to stop working as soon as you figure them out. Paid advertising produces mixed results, and it gets very difficult to predict and replicate success if you don't know the underlying reason for *why* something works well or fails dismally.

Ultimately, failing to attract your dream client by designing the wrong types of people into your business hinders your capacity to live a balanced, financially free life doing something you love.

In this topsy-turvy, reactional model of running a 'yes-first' business, every shiny marketing solution can fall flat, because you don't know who you're trying to speak to, how to reach the right prospects, or what to say to people when the occasional dream client happens to fall from the sky!

But here's a well-kept secret. Marketing doesn't need to be this hard.

What if we could look at the perfect client base, take it apart to see how it was formed, and recreate the same process in your business to make the ideal client base for you?

This is reverse-engineered marketing in action. We're looking at the ideal result, taking it apart to see how it's achieved, and then applying the right processes to design the same result into your marketing strategy.

REVERSE-ENGINEERING DREAM CLIENTS INTO YOUR BUSINESS FROM THE OUTSET IS A NO-BRAINER.

Let's pause for a moment and consider the untapped potential of our clients, good or bad, in a different kind of way.

If we attract the clients that we design into our business whether we mean to or not, then we can intentionally design only the clients we *do* want into our business strategy right from the outset.

Just because you can do something for your less-than-perfect client, doesn't mean you should.

Getting that right is nothing more than understanding what the dream client looks like, and coming up with a set of clear communication strategies that can design the right path from their juicy problem straight to your open door.

When you have quality clients who properly get what you do, you can deliver your best for them, because when we like our clients, we go to great lengths to serve them. This grows your reputation.

With Enriched Marketing, every client you work with naturally sets you up for success, because they're already a good fit for your best solution.

Working with clients who help you succeed means work becomes more enjoyable and less emotionally draining. This enhanced energy leads to better output, which grows your revenue with predictable results, and brings more of the good clients into your business.

In this model, your success is based on understanding the reason why your business is working the way it should. This sets you up for further success, and scales your business for the easy-going, financially free future you really want, without compromising on your ability to have an impact on the people you serve.

Choosing to only fill your client base with people who help you succeed in your business allows you to work less, because you're not wasting time on people who don't add value. It empowers you to charge more for your services too, because your solution brings enviable results.

Most importantly, designing the ideal client into your business strategy gives you the confidence to thrive in the business landscape. This alone is one of the most powerful factors in building a successful, profitable brand.

With confidence comes results. With results comes profit. With profit comes the freedom to apply your time to the things you like best.

Why waste time and resources on guesswork, when you can just as easily decide who you want to work with and fill your client base with only those types of people?

Over the coming pages, I'll share with you what I've learned through working closely with my own dream clients, as well as with the types of clients who should never have made it into my client base. Bad clients have taught me the most valuable lessons in learning to say no.

Every day, I develop powerful marketing communication campaigns that scale profit, reduce complexity, and pull the right types of dream clients into highly successful brands.

This book exists so that you don't have to figure out the chaos in your own marketing. You don't need to tire yourself out chasing the wrong prospects around the barren wilderness with your 'pick-me' hat on, hoping they might say yes to you one day. You can just read this book, enrich your marketing, and set yourself apart.

I'm here to give you a shortcut to emotional marketing techniques that always work, because they're derived from the deep psychology that makes us inherently human.

Throughout my 20-plus-year career in sales and marketing, I've helped businesses across the world to elevate their brand stories, boost sales, and win their dream clients' hearts by flipping conventional business building on its ear.

My life's work is to craft masterful sales strategies that design dream clients into powerful marketing campaigns using simple human psychology. I'm passionate about pulling the right strings to inspire meaningful change, with profit-driven results.

What you'll learn in this book is not reliant on changing times or modern technology. The strategies you'll discover here exist with or without the internet. They're based on theories of fundamental human nature that have been around for generations of decision-making societies.

Human nature is the inherent process by which we collectively live and share our lives with others.

My goal is to step away from the marketing jargon and misconceptions that business owners run into by default, and recreate something that's *fundamentally better* by design. I'm here to unpack your dream scenario, and to help you reverse-engineer high-quality clients into your business design with powerful communication strategies that prove their success time and time again.

If you put in the effort to design your dream clients into your business, then you can expect to fill your calendar with the very best clients who *want* to pay a premium price just for the opportunity to choose you.*

When you design these premium clients into your business, and when the right types of people start resonating with you, then your dream clients will seek you out and come to you. This achieves the gold standard of attraction marketing that's used by the top slice of the world's most successful brands.

The secrets you'll unwrap in this book mean you can finally stop chasing dead leads, and start living the luxury life of lattes and long walks on the beach. Instagram optional.

Enriched Marketing will open dream opportunities for you to *only* work with the good clients that *you* want to work with, doing things you love to achieve the very best results for the people you most want to help – without running your tail off.

But first, you must do the work, and you must do it well.

What you'll learn in these pages is not how to entice people with *yet another launch* that will somehow be better than the last 20 launches you did. Nor will you learn how to outsmart AI, make people less critical, or beat the ever-changing 'algorithm' – international bot of mystery.

'The algorithm' is just a blanket term used in marketing that describes decisions made by a robot, where ordinary working humans have no proper insight into how those decisions are actually made.

---

* Throughout this book, I use the terms 'clients' and 'customers', as well as 'products' and 'services', interchangeably. This ultimately boils down to the people who pay you, and the things they pay you for. While this book is predominately geared towards businesses that offer a service as the primary product, the principles of human psychology in sales and marketing apply to all businesses in all industries, regardless of what you sell or who you sell it to.

Instead, I'll show you a sophisticated system for leveraging the power of human psychology in sales and marketing.

When you get that right, all the other sparkly things that marketing books promise can fall into place naturally. This happens because you start engaging with real people who love your style, which moves you up Google's rankings and helps your brand to grow with authenticity and true integrity.

We'll figure out who the dream client is at a deeply human level and define which of your services will resonate with them. We'll unpack their emotional drivers, and we'll craft a meaningful collection of key messages that will encourage these dream clients to come to you, because they recognise that *you* can help them in a meaningful way.

When you win people's hearts, they give you their minds, and with that, they nearly always give you their money too.

Sales and marketing are neither complicated nor difficult if you're selling the right stuff to the right types of people. This book will teach you how to understand who the right types of people are, what you should be selling to them, and how you can win their hearts to also win more sales.

Before we start, I would like you to do this quick, 5-minute exercise, using no more than 1 minute per question.

We're going to come back to these same questions later in this book, so write your answers down and keep them safe.

Don't overthink it!

1. What do you do?

2. Why are you qualified to do that?

3. Why do people like you?

4. Why do people struggle to solve the thing you solve?

5. Who is your target client?

Ready?

Let's make some magic!

SECTION 1

START WITH THE END IN MIND

CHAPTER 1

TWO SIDES TO SELLING WITH CARE

'People don't care how much you know until they know how much you care.' - Theodore Roosevelt, former US president

F OR a few years in my late 20s, I travelled the world as a luxury cruise ship photographer. Each week, we received 2,000 new guests into a wash-rinse-repeat-style sales environment located at sea, in a floating hotel.

As a team, we snapped event-style photos of the guests on their cruises, taking the same photographs on the same days of the week, in the same studio locations, using the same format. We sold them in the same photo gallery, open at the same hours, using the same production process…

You get the picture.

Guests were offered a choice of whether or not they would

like to have their photo taken, and if they chose to allow a photo, they were under no obligation to buy it. We printed them all, displayed them in the photo gallery, and sold them for $20 or $40 respectively, depending on the picture size.

As the department head, I ran a photo lab and a sales lab. The only variables that ever changed in the sales lab were the guests in our audience. Everything else was a constant.

This was an ideal test-tube opportunity to run live A/B testing* on real humans, so naturally, I did what all good sales managers do and kept a spreadsheet of tiny changes to see how measurable tweaks in the way we communicated our value impacted our sales.

If we put the pictures over there, do the sales go up? If we change red signs to blue signs, do the sales go up? If we wait a day before displaying the smaller prints, do the sales go up?

Most cruise ship guests decide before they arrive that they don't want pictures. Many have drawers full of ship photos gathering dust at home, and nearly all would prefer not to stop for a picture when they're late for a show, heading to catch a shore excursion, or simply tired of people sticking cameras in their faces.

Cruise ship photos are perceived to be overpriced, inconvenient, and most of the time neither a want nor a need to the average cruise ship guest. So why then did these same guests who didn't want our service buy thousands of dollars' worth of pictures in our gallery each week?

---

* A/B testing, you simply look at two variables of the same thing, then choose the one that's most successful with your target audience.

Quite simply, because people are human, and humans can be easily persuaded into doing things they don't think they should do.

Working on cruise ships was a real-life boot camp for the online sales environments we have today.

The lessons I learned from selling pop-up studio portraits on cruise ships were nothing more than lessons of human attachment. People don't buy photographs. They buy how the photographer makes them feel when the photo is taken.

I recognised early on that people only bought the photos when the photographers captured the way they saw themselves – when they caught something close to that idealistic image we hold in our heads of who we are on our best days. So instead of running special promos in the gallery to boost sales, we instead focused on building rapport in our studios to help people feel more comfortable with the concept of ship photography.

When the guests saw the photographer had captured them the way they saw themselves, their own self-recognition meant they grew attached to the images when they held them in their hands, so we changed our in-gallery sales strategy too.

Instead of asking people if they *liked* the photos displayed on the wall, we simply placed the prints into their hands and let them decide for themselves if they wanted to buy a memory of the way the photographer had made them feel on the day.

During my 4-year tenure, we sold more than 5 million dollars worth of photos to people who were adamantly sure they didn't want their pictures taken.

Selling with care follows the same philosophy.

SECRET #1
SELLING WITH CARE IS ABOUT MAKING OTHER PEOPLE FEEL GOOD.

The first side of selling with care says that if you care enough to help your clients feel good when they interact with your business, then your ideal client will buy into your concept and say yes to you. This happens even if they're not really in the market for whatever you think they need, and even if they've already decided that they definitely *don't want* whatever it is you're selling.

People recognise things that reflect themselves, and they'll only buy something when they see something of themselves reflected in their purchase decision.

If a person identifies as having an arty nature, and they buy something from a company that feels arty, they will see themselves reflected in the purchase. Likewise, if somebody likes things to be in neat little boxes, they will feel the purchase reflects who they are when they buy things that come in neat little boxes.

Post-it Notes are a great example of this. To some, the tiny notes are completely useless because they don't give us enough space to write freely. To others, the tiny notes are genius, because they box ideas into neat little squares.

Self-identification plays a significant role in the success of a sale. People who feel seen for who they are say, 'Yes, I like this because it represents me.'

This is an essential concept that we'll keep coming back to because the only way to sell successfully is to ensure your buyers can see themselves in your story at a deep psychological level, just like the cruise ship guests could see themselves the way they wanted to be seen in the photos they thought they didn't want.

It's also a concept that most businesses get wrong from the outset, because the average business owner doesn't think about the underlying psychology of their dream client before building their brand.

In Enriched Marketing, the customer is always at the heart of the brand story. Without the customer, the reverse-engineered brand story cannot exist, so the customer's deep psychological needs must come first.

We must care about the customer's success above all else.

The mistake most business owners make is they focus on the business idea first, then build the brand they want to be, and figure out who their ideal client is once the business is built. In this upside-down way of thinking, the desired client is last to the party and becomes something of an afterthought.

With this approach of building the business first and then trying to find customers for it, there is a fundamental misalignment between what the business wants to be, and who the business is trying to sell to.

In Enriched Marketing, the dream client must be the foundation block around which everything else springs to life. When we make it about them, they buy into us.

Secret #2

Selling with care is about caring who you sell to.

The second element in selling with care is about caring who you sell to. It means choosing your clients wisely and learning to say no to the people who aren't a perfect fit for your business.

Saying no can be hard to do sometimes, but learning to turn work down is the game-changing moment between being an 'always-say-yes' reactive business and a proactive brand that puts customer success at the heart of the story.

Successful businesses must be exceptionally picky about who is allowed into the business ecosystem, and which types of people are invited to become paying clients, because the success of the customer defines the success of the brand. When they thrive, you thrive, so the best way to get ahead is to focus only on the people who you know you can help to thrive.

Most businesses are started a little like this:

Let's say for the moment that you're a graphic designer with additional skills in social media, copywriting, and website development. You have strong skills in a few different areas, with a burning desire to create high-profile marketing collateral for large-scale sports events. That's a niche market, with a generalised set of creative skills. On paper, it should be successful.

On day one, you have no clients because your business is new. Using conventional entrepreneurial thinking, you might start by telling a few people in your network that you're a freelance graphic designer. Perhaps you create a profile on Upwork or Fiverr, and attend a few networking groups or promote yourself on LinkedIn. Eventually, someone asks you to design a logo, so you celebrate and get your first paying client.

When the next client chooses you, they see you design logos, so they book you for their logo and perhaps also ask you to create some social media content. The next client sees you do social media content, so they ask if you can make a whole website for them. You say yes, because you're designing things and you're not a bad writer, so why not just wing it and do the whole lot for all of the money?

This process works well for a time. Your business grows, and you earn a reputation as a talented graphic designer who also helps with social media, websites, and copywriting. Small business owners love you!

Every day, you work on a variety of scattered projects that all ask for something unique. Every day is a fresh, oftentimes steep learning curve, but you never manage to deepen your portfolio with the things you really want.

Fast forward ten years and your business is filled with low-ball clients who milk your energy because they can't afford to hire multiple freelancers, while other, more-experienced niche designers get to create high-profile sports collateral for the large-scale clients that you never seem to land.

Following conventional advice for building a business has failed, because you didn't start with the end in mind. You ran for the shiny things that looked good on the day and ended up with a different type of business to the one you first dreamed of. Maybe it's not a bad business, and maybe you've grown to like it, but it's not the one you wanted, and that's *always* an unseen booby prize.

I started two businesses like this. Both failed in the first year. Now I work four hours a day, spend next to nothing on ads, and run a six-week waiting list that can be switched on or off whenever I choose.

Why? Because I only work with the people who can set me up for success, and those people are the ones who bring both money and joy into my business. For the rest, I just say no.

Caring who you sell to is imperative in Enriched Marketing, because it places the dream client at the heart of the story, and everybody else is nothing more than a distraction from your customer's success story.

When bad clients become a distraction, it takes away from your ability to serve good clients properly using your best efforts. Every bad client who saps your energy diminishes the energy you can give to a good client.

In short, too many incompatible clients can easily cause a business to deliver bad service to good clients, which can harm your reputation and lead your good clients to seek your solutions elsewhere.

The same rings true for every industry.

If you've built your business using reactive techniques that always say yes, then chances are, your dream clients are out there waiting for you on somebody else's silver spoon. You just need to reach out and take them.

Carefully selecting your client base and choosing your work wisely opens your energy and makes you wholly available to the people you are most equipped to get results for. These dream clients are glad to have the opportunity to pay your premium rates, just so they can choose you over your competition.

But remember that every business is different. You'll need to decide for yourself when you can start turning away bad clients based on your own cash flow, and your own personal situation. My advice is to do it as soon as you can, within a comfortable financial timeframe.

In the coming pages, I'll show you how to unpack the dream client, so you can design the right people into your business ecosystem with caring intent.

KEY TAKEAWAYS

Selling with care has two essential elements:

1. We must care deeply for the people we serve.

2. We must be selective about the types of clients we work with.

Every client you work with must recognise your ability to help them at a deep psychological level.

The dream client must always be at the heart of your business. When you build the business around the dream client, the dream client buys into your brand's philosophy, and resonates with your brand story.

A reverse-engineered brand story attracts your target clients towards you, and inspires their yes response.

To attract dream clients who value what you do and who want to pay a premium price for the opportunity to work with you, you must first start with the end in mind, and then reverse-engineer your ideal clients into your business by design.

Learn to say no to bad clients. Start saying no as early as possible.

CHAPTER 2

WHAT ARE REVERSE-ENGINEERED BRAND STORIES?

'The greatest mistake marketers make is trying to create demand.' - Eugene Schwartz, Breakthrough Advertising

TIME and time again, I see business owners who come up with an idea, decide what they like about it, then head out into the world of potential prospects and try to drum up demand for it.

This is the equivalent of standing on a busy shopping street in the heart of a major city with a box of beetroot-flavoured cupcakes, and encouraging people to want to buy them.

A beetroot-flavoured cupcake seller on London's Oxford Street will certainly sell some cupcakes, but only to people who care enough to stop. Even when they do stop, the only people who will actually buy the cupcakes are people who already understand the value of beetroot and already like the idea of putting it in a cupcake.

Everybody else will just walk by, or they'll buy a more familiar chocolate cupcake from somewhere else, because no matter how hard you try, you can't *make* people want to eat a beetroot cupcake. This is true even if *you* know they're nice to eat, and even if the people walking past you are desperately hungry for cupcakes.

A better solution would be to place your box of beetroot cupcakes in a popular bakery that specialises in unusual cupcakes. With this approach, you're only trying to sell beetroot cupcakes to people who already want an unusually flavoured cupcake, so your job becomes much simpler.

They're already there waiting to buy what you have, so all you need to do is show them why they'll like your beetroot cupcake more than your competitor's rhubarb cupcake and show them where to pay for it.

This is much easier than trying to get a wide variety of people on a busy shopping street to notice you, let alone buy something from your little box of weird food.

Now, that's all good and well if you're selling in person. When you sell online, you're always just going to be 'on the internet', and the internet doesn't have nice, neat little silos where people can sell cupcakes in bakeries.

People browsing online all start their search in the same place – on the internet's search bar, which is the same sales arena for all businesses in all industries.

Selling online is always the equivalent of standing with a box of cupcakes on a busy street corner, so you need to be very clever about how you dress and what you say, so that all the people who want beetroot cupcakes seek you out as the perfect cupcake seller.

Your brand story is what allows you to gather people who share your values into a carved-out corner of the internet. It's the equivalent of moving your cupcake box into a specialist shop where people already get what you do.

At its heart, Enriched Marketing answers the question, 'How do we fill our business ecosystem with the people we want to sell to (those interested in beetroot cupcakes), and filter out the people we don't want to sell to (everybody else)?'

In other words:

How do we take the whole internet's worth of cold prospects with low-level awareness and convert them into valuable clients who want to pay a premium price just for the opportunity to choose you?

It may sound like magic, but it's definitely not! Reverse-engineering is the secret strategy used by the world's best marketers.

The biggest and best brands don't just talk about themselves or their products and services. They celebrate the pinnacles of greatness. They inspire people to believe in the impossible. They showcase the successes of people who look like their dream clients.

On Coca-Cola's own website, the only thing it says about Coke is that it's 'The World's Favourite Soft Drink.'* They don't need to talk about how it's made or what it tastes like. That

---

* https://www.yourcoca-cola.co.uk/brands/coca-cola-original-taste.list, correct at the time of writing. Powerhouse brands constantly tweak and refine their website messaging to match their customers' changing needs, so if it's changed by the time you read this book, it will likely be something equally effective.

statement is enough to make people who agree with the sentiment feel like they want to be part of the Coke-drinking community.

If you don't agree that Coke is the world's favourite soft drink, then you probably won't buy Coke from the website or in your favourite restaurant.

The world's most successful brands know *precisely* how their dream clients will respond to certain scenarios, so they plant the correct messages in all the right places to entice the desired response from the people they most want a response from.

This is reverse-engineered marketing in action. When brands like Nike celebrate great athletics, people who want to be great athletes buy their products. It makes a natural connection between the best athletes and the best running shoes.

Reverse-engineering in marketing is all about creating emotional forces in the underlying psychology of the target consumer. When we tap into the forces of human nature to uncover our existing desires, we can drive significant growth.

Decades of research into the emerging neuroscience of intrinsic motivation[*] – the stuff that's built into our hardwiring and guides our decisions – shows that people are compelled to make choices according to their natural preferences for psychological wellness.

For example, if a person is intrinsically motivated by their psychological need for independence, then the significant choices

---

[*] Domenico, S. and Ryan, R. (2017) 'The emerging neuroscience of intrinsic motivation: A new frontier in self-determination research', Frontiers in Human Neuroscience, 11, doi:10.3389/fnhum.2017.00145.

they make in life will generally move them towards finding their independence.

When somebody is psychologically motivated by their intrinsic need for belonging, they will seek social bonds wherever they can.

If you frame your brand story within the context of this deep psychology, then the right people will come running towards you, because they recognise that you can help them to achieve their psychological wellness.

This is so important to get right. If you build a brand that delivers the wrong psychological benefits, then you'll accidentally design the wrong types of people into your business, and your business will surely fail even if your USPs say that you're faster, better, or more effective than your many competitors.

In Enriched Marketing, your USPs don't actually matter much, because your USPs are mostly all about you, and interested people are far more interested in what you can say about them than they'll ever be in what you can say about yourself. The only thing that matters is the dream client's psychological profile, and the emotional brand story you create to trigger them into action.

One of the best examples of reverse-engineering for Enriched Marketing is Apple's 'Think Different' campaign.*

Just before this campaign was launched, Apple was struggling along as the somewhat misunderstood second-choice computer

---

* Siltanen, R. (2011) 'The real story behind Apple's 'Think different' campaign', *Forbes*, 14 December. Available at: https://www.forbes.com/sites/onmarketing/2011/12/14/the-real-story-behind-apples-think-different-campaign/?sh=2242ed3762ab

company standing in the shadow of Microsoft. It was destined for those who beat to their own drums while the rest of the world used Microsoft.

Apple didn't want the same pot of standard clients that Microsoft was competing for, so they called out their own dream client as the rebel. An outlaw who believes they can change the world.

Rebels are psychologically motivated by their desire to leave their mark on the world. They want to break the mould and be remembered for doing the unexpected. The emotional trigger for a rebel is being perceived as ordinary.

Apple calls out their dream client in a single paragraph by referencing all the things that outlaws seek at a deep psychological level. This frames Apple as a place where conformity doesn't need to exist.

Steve Jobs' voiceover is placed over a series of video clips of people who have somehow changed the world. Great rebel minds used include the likes of Albert Einstein, Martin Luther King Jr, John Lennon, and Amelia Earhart. The script reads:

> 'Here's to the crazy ones, the misfits, the rebels, the troublemakers, the round pegs in square holes. The ones who see things differently – they're not fond of rules. You can quote them, disagree with them, glorify or vilify them, but the only thing you can't do is ignore them. Because they change things. They push the human race forward, and while some may see them as the crazy ones, we see

genius, because the ones who are crazy enough to think that they can change the world, are the ones who do.'

– Steve Jobs, 1997

Using the very same principles that you'll learn in this book, Apple quietly slipped the right psychological triggers into their brand story to attract people who don't want to be seen as ordinary, and knocked their competition right out of the park!

At the time of writing this book, Apple remains the world's biggest brand, delivering annual revenues with a surplus of $275 billion worldwide, which was grown from a small cult following of devout dream clients who self-identified as going against the grain.

Not once does Apple mention the USPs of their products in their ad campaign.

They're Apple; they sell Apple products to people who feel inspired by those who change the world. People who buy Apple products want Apple products because they would like to leave their mark too.

Most Apple users can't tell you how their iPhone is better than every Android on the market; they just know that it is better because that's what they want to believe when they decide to buy from Apple.

Off the back of the 'Think Different' campaign, today's Apple users are willing to pay premium prices to be part of the club of rebel minds who believe their ability to think differently sets them apart.

Apple users need to feel distinguished, and that's a deep psychological need that will never be extinguished. For as long as

Apple continues to make Apple users feel like they're a cut above, they will continue to attract loyal customers who self-recognise their desire to set themselves apart and change the world.

You can test this in real life.

Next time you see an Apple user, ask them why they choose Apple. They'll likely just tell you they're an 'Apple person'. Next time you see an Android user, ask them why they don't have Apple. They'll likely tell you they don't like how Apple's captive ecosystem doesn't work well with their other devices.

Rebel customers want to break the status quo, so they willingly buy into Apple's outlaw brand, and wouldn't have it any other way.

A similar brand story rivalry exists between Coca-Cola and Pepsi. People who drink Coke often don't like Pepsi on principle. It's fundamentally the same product – a fizzy, cola-flavoured soft drink – so why should this be?

THE BRAND STORY DETERMINES THE CUSTOMER.

As we now know, the USPs separating the two rival brands are irrelevant.

What matters is the people at the heart of their brand stories, and how the two brands have reverse-engineered these people into their brand messaging.

For both brands, the dream client is driven by their deep psychological need for belonging. However, Pepsi's dream customers want to live in the moment and see the funny side of life, while Coke's ideal customers want to share meaningful moments with others.

Pepsi creates a sense of belonging in the Pepsi club by poking fun at high-profile situations. This reverse-engineers people who buy through humour into their brand story.

When David Beckham was famously sent off for kicking out at Diego Simeone during the 1998 Men's Football World Cup, Pepsi released a short television ad to poke fun at him.

In the advert, David Beckham was shown in the corridor off the pitch feeling deflated by his red card. A young girl asks if she can have his shirt, which instantly lightens the mood as he dramatically takes it off his back to give it to her. She uses it to wipe the top of her Pepsi can and gives the dirty shirt back to him.

Contrary to this tongue-in-cheek brand story, Coke is a celebration of the human spirit. From seeing Father Christmas arrive in the iconic red truck, to making homemade pasta with old friends, the story of Coca-Cola brings people together with generosity and kindness.

Which you prefer to drink is not so much a matter of taste or their USPs, but a sense of alignment with the brand story.

If Coca-Cola suddenly started poking fun at famous people, they would start to lose their loyal customers. If Pepsi stopped joking around, they would lose theirs too.

The USPs for Apple, Pepsi and Coca-Cola are irrelevant. What matters is the people who have been reverse-engineered into their long-term brand stories: dream clients!

Each one of these highly successful global brands has intentionally designed the types of customers they want into their business from the outset using reverse-engineered brand storytelling.

Not all clients are meant to be yours. The more you can filter out the ones that work against you, the easier it becomes to magnetise the finest clients right to your door.

Apple has such a strong loyalty that anybody who isn't willing to switch to Apple's captive ecosystem is actively encouraged to stick to Android. They're not a good fit for Apple's overall business model, so these kinds of people who aren't willing to go all-in get a big fat no (subtly, of course).

Saying no to the ordinary is what enables Apple to be Apple. The people who shy away from ordinary will beat to their own drums as die-hard Apple fans, and will never have it any other way.

People who drink Coke will nearly always order something else if the restaurant only stocks Pepsi. Restaurants that stock Pepsi hardly ever have Coke.

Powerful stuff!

Key takeaways

In Enriched Marketing, the business USPs are largely irrelevant. What matters are the underlying psychological needs of the target client.

Reverse-engineering brand stories is about pairing deep psychological needs with strong emotional stories that resonate with dream clients.

The biggest brands on the planet thrive because they started with the end in mind, then filled their customer base with only the types of people who naturally relate to their brand stories. The most successful brands attract the right types of people into their business ecosystems by design, so they don't need to create demand for their products and services.

The desired customer must always be at the heart of your business.

CHAPTER 3

BE THE BRIDGE

*'Remember the people you address are selfish,
as we all are. They care nothing about your interests
or profit. They seek service for themselves. Ignoring this
fact is a common mistake and a costly mistake
in advertising.'* - Claude C. Hopkins, *Scientific Advertising*

To create a compelling reverse-engineered brand story, we need to get to know our desired clients at a deep psychological level a long time before we start trying to sell to them. We need to understand their selfish desires, so we can leverage them to our advantage.

There are four elements that work together to build your reverse-engineered brand story. All four elements are essential because they each turn a small cog in a giant wheel. This what drives the sales to increase profitability in your business.

We'll look at each element in detail in the coming chapters, but for now, let's connect the dots using big-picture thinking.

- Firstly, we need to understand the dream client's deep psychological profile. What do they respond to, and what are they motivated by in their subconscious?

- Next, we'll map their key emotional drivers. What do they really want, and what are they afraid of?

- Then, we'll unpack the changing levels of awareness in your audience. How much do they know about their problem, and how can we move them closer towards you as their awareness grows?

- Finally, we'll create a tailored brand language that resonates with the dream client's emotional story to decide which specific words will inspire them to act.

Once we have a clear strategy for how to design the dream client into your brand story, we'll use the brand story to create compelling sales copy and other important communication channels for your business.

Before we get started with that, let's take a moment to understand how this all fits together, and why every component of the reverse-engineered brand story matters in Enriched Marketing.

Remember, our job at this stage is not to sell to people, it's just to create a business ecosystem that gives you the right people to sell to. We're creating a bakery that specialises in unusual cupcakes, so we can place our beetroot cupcakes into the right target market for a successful outcome.

Imagine for a moment that everybody who shares the common problem you solve is grouped together onto a single island, where they feel confused, frustrated, and ready to make a change to solve their problem.

Let's call this island the land of darkness and confusion. Here, everybody is struggling with the same general problem, but nothing differentiates them from each other. This is a big island filled with generalised prospects, where you can potentially 'help everybody' because your product is just that good.

Surrounding the island of darkness and confusion are many islands of light and joy. These islands represent you, and also your competitors. Each island promises a solution to the common problem, but only to the people who come to an island of light and joy to receive it.

Marketing is the process of bringing people from the land of darkness and confusion to your land of light and joy. When people arrive on your island, you can sell your service to them.

Your brand story is the bridge that links the place of problem to the place of solution – the land of darkness and confusion to the land of light and joy. Your brand story needs to encourage people to choose your island over other competing islands, and it needs to make sure that only the right types of people come to your island.

If everybody crosses the bridge to your island, then your island just becomes a different version of the land of darkness and confusion. We only want some people to come to our island, and we want to be choosy about who those people are.

Remember, you don't want to sell to everybody. You only want to sell to the people who you know will set you up for success. To achieve that, you need to design an island that's filled with dream clients, and *only* with dream clients.

Reverse-engineering your brand story is the process of building the right bridge, so that *only* the right types of people choose to come to your island. Your brand story is the bridge. Enriched Marketing creates a bridge and moves people along it so that you can sell to them effortlessly when they arrive at your business door, on the island of light and joy.

This intentional island design creates a pool of high-value prospects who appreciate what you do, recognise that you can help them, and feel compelled to buy into your business because their deep psychological needs are met.

When your island is filled with these people, the sales conversions skyrocket, profits soar, and the loyalty these people feel to your business becomes immeasurable.

For the rest of this book, everything we talk about will be geared towards asking the right people to step onto your bridge, then moving them through their various layers of consumer awareness, until they reach a place where you can sell to them.

Once your brand story is in place, all you need to do is sit on your island and shine your authentic light. The dream client will come to you because they want to be part of your brand story. This client is gold dust, and in the big picture, this client is the only one you want.

A QUICK EXERCISE

Answer the below questions in just a few words using a minute or two per question. Your goal at this stage is to develop a clear image in your mind of the land of darkness and the land of light, using a very broad brushstroke.

- Which industry do you work in?

- What is the common problem your current clients face?

- What do you fundamentally solve for your current clients?

- What is your solution to their common problem?

For example, you may answer these questions like this:

- Which industry do you work in? Travel industry.

- What is the common problem your current clients face? They don't know where to go on holiday.

- What do you solve for your current clients? I help them decide where to go on holiday.

- What is your solution to their common problem? Travel planning.

Try not to overthink your answers. You just want to create a clear picture.

In the travel industry example above, the land of darkness and confusion is filled with people who don't know where to go on their holidays.

The land of light and joy is a place where these decisions are made for you, with the help of travel planning services.

A NOTE ON ETHICS

The techniques you'll learn in this book are powerful. When you master these skills, you'll have the capacity to direct and steer people to behave the way you want them to.

A few years ago, I was working with one of my mentees, Elizabeth, to develop her sales techniques. As I was running through the process for removing client objections, we spoke about delivering information using a closed-open question.

A closed-open question is a question where you ask somebody for their input in a way that subconsciously persuades them to give the answer you want them to give. Card tricksters, magicians, and marketers all use a similar 'sleight of hand' to entice the right response from an audience.

Elizabeth rightly asked me where the line gets drawn between persuasion in sales and outright manipulation, because manipulating people is generally considered to be unethical in life and business.

This is an excellent question, and it comes down to the integrity of the marketer's intention.

Sales, persuasion, and reverse-engineered brand storytelling puts the client at the heart of the business. The business exists to serve the dream client, and is always guided by the success of the client. This is ethical, because you're always acting in the client's best interest, and doing everything you can to give them a positive experience with your brand.

Manipulation is self-serving. This is unethical, and it doesn't work in sales, because it puts the business first and doesn't care how the business affects the customer. Manipulation in marketing is the root cause of why people lose fortunes buying into scams and other dubious services.

The techniques are the same, but the intention behind why we use them is different, and this comes down to your personal and business integrity.

Ultimately, you need to draw the line yourself, but please use this knowledge responsibly. Understanding psychological selling is a formidable tool that applies to life and business in equal measure.

These techniques should always and only be used for the right reasons – to attract, help and serve your dream clients, so you can grow your business with authentic integrity.

Sell with care!

CHAPTER 4

FINDING YOUR BUSINESS SUPERPOWER

'Don't believe what your eyes are telling you.
All they show is limitation. Look with your understanding.
Find out what you already know and you will see the
way to fly.' – Richard Bach, *Jonathan Livingston Seagull*

I've said previously that your unique selling points (USPs) are largely irrelevant in relation to your dream client's needs, but you still need to know what your business actually does before you can start thinking about who the ideal client is.

Knowing your USPs and knowing what your business does are two completely different things.

What you do in your business can be understood as: 'Which common problem do you solve, using which solution?' USPs, however, can be understood as: 'What makes you different to your competitors who offer the same solution to the same common problem?'

What your business does focuses on what you do for the customer. What makes you special focuses on you. Selfish customers don't care about you, they care about what you do for them.

USPs are largely irrelevant in marketing because how you differ from your competitors doesn't actually matter to your customers. What matters to them is whether or not you understand how to meet their underlying psychological needs, and whether or not they align with your brand story.

In Enriched Marketing, your USPs don't feature much. If you get the story right, people will choose you regardless of what sets you apart from your competitors. If you get the story wrong, people will turn away from you even if your list of USPs is as long as your arm.

To look at this a slightly different way, if people have a deep psychological need for freedom, then they don't care if your getaway car is red or blue. They care only that your getaway car will be their ticket to freedom.

In this scenario, your business superpower is your ability to give people their freedom. Your USP is the colour of your getaway car. You need to know what your business superpower is before you can work out who the dream client is, but your USP doesn't have any real impact on your brand story, so you don't need to worry about what sets you apart for now.

So, let's start with the end in mind to find your business superpower.

Creating an end-in-mind vision of the perfect business is just the culmination of two essential things:

1. What do people need your help with (what's their common problem)?

2. How can you best help them (what's your fundamental solution)?

To answer this properly, we need to find your Ikigai – *your reason for being.* Why does your business exist?

Ikigai is an ancient Japanese concept that dates all the way back to the Heian period from 784 to 1185. It refers to the singular moment when everything falls into place. In Japanese culture, when you find your Ikigai, you find your greater purpose, which facilitates living a meaningful life.

In business, your business superpower is the Ikigai moment when the reason your business exists falls into place.

Ikigai is a reason for being that inspires greatness in yourself and others.

The concept of Ikigai is at the heart of meaningful business design, and later forms the cornerstone of your premium offer. It answers the question, 'Where do you ultimately want your business to go, and what would you like people to buy from you in the perfect scenario?'

Think about the business you would like to create, or where you would like to steer your existing business to in the future.

There are four questions you must answer in depth to find your business superpower.

1. WHAT CAN YOU DO FOR PEOPLE?

This covers your full wheelhouse of skills. If you're a service business, what does your collection of specialist knowledge and skills look like, and what can you achieve with it? If you're a product business, what does your full catalogue of viable products include?

For the next three to five minutes, use a large piece of paper to brainstorm everything you can do for your clients. Separate complex services into multiple items, so that every item on your page consists of just one product or service, with one concept and one result.

For example, if you're a graphic designer, you'll separate 'creating brand identity' into logo design, stationery design, and choosing brand colour palettes. If you're an executive coach, you'll separate people development into goal setting, team morale, and profit strategies. If you sell fitness products, you'll separate protein shakes, snack bars, and energy drinks into separate products.

This list should include everything that you're capable of delivering. You're looking to make the biggest list possible, so just brain-dump everything you can think of that falls under the category 'things I can offer in my business' into your list.

This broad list should include everything that you *can* offer, regardless of whether or not you already offer the product or service to your existing clients.

When you think your list is finished, go into it again and expand your ideas out into more ideas, until you have found everything you have in your wheelhouse.

2. WHAT DO YOU ENJOY DOING?

In 2019, The Telegraph reported that 60% of new businesses fail within the first three years.* This is oftentimes a direct result of building a reactive business that fails to attract the right client base to be successful.

Reactive thinking accidentally designs the wrong types of clients into the business ecosystem because people who use this methodology are nearly always trying to create demand within their chosen target markets. Businesses that react to unpredictable demand tend to rely on the 'always-say-yes' response to keep new clients flowing through the door.

As we know, the wrong types of clients will ask for things that take extra resources to accommodate and don't always make us happy. In reactive marketing, we know it's not a good fit, but we say yes anyway, because we're scared to lose the sale, and we're never sure where the next client will come from.

---

* May, R. (2019) 'Start-ups across the UK are going bust: They need more careful management for our economy to boom', The Telegraph, 24 January. Available at:https://www.telegraph.co.uk/politics/2019/01/24/start-ups-across-uk-going-bust-need-careful-management-economy/

If you want your dream clients to bring you money and joy in equal measure, then it's essential that you only offer a collection of products and services that bring you both joy and money.

Go through your list of the things you can do, and cross off everything that doesn't make you happy, and everything that isn't easily profitable.

The goal of this exercise is to eliminate all of the products and services that don't contribute towards your dream business, so be ruthless! You want to make your long list as short as possible.

If it doesn't make you happy, and if you don't enjoy doing something as much as you know you should, then take it off your list.

At this stage, you may be surprised to find that your shortened list includes some unexpected items, and has eliminated some things you thought you could never get rid of. Embrace your courage, and refine your list as much as you can!

3. WHAT DO PEOPLE NEED YOU TO DO FOR THEM?

You can't create demand where demand doesn't exist, but you can activate demand when people have low awareness and don't yet know *why* they need your solution to their problem – or perhaps don't yet know that they have a problem at all!

Think about the things that people already ask you for, and also think about any gaps in your market that are not currently filled. Think too about your competitors.

What do other people offer? How do others achieve success in your industry?

It's no use flogging a dead horse that nobody needs, so go back through your list again and remove anything that is obviously not needed in your area of expertise, and also anything that doesn't naturally self-identify as a clear opportunity in your wider market.

For example, if nobody is selling ice to people who live in the Arctic then it's likely because people in the Arctic don't need ice, and there is no demand for ice shops in a frozen environment.

If you're selling convenient fitness products, then there may not be a need for individual smoothie ingredients if people are already able to buy pre-mixed smoothie packs for the same cost.

Our goal here is to make sure that you have a genuine opportunity to do business with your preferred collection of products and services.

A top tip is to eliminate everything that you don't naturally excel at. If you know you're not competitive on skill or quality, then just take it off the list and focus on what you are good at.

4. WHAT ARE PEOPLE WILLING TO PAY YOU FOR?

By now, your list should only include the items that satisfy all three of the previous criteria: they should be possible, enjoyable, and genuinely needed by some people, regardless of the pre-existing market awareness.

Remember, low awareness can often indicate a gap in the

market, so don't worry if you don't get actively asked for something on your list. If it self-identifies as a valuable market gap, you have a winner!

The last step in finding your Ikigai is simply to check that people are willing to pay for everything on your list. A good way to do this is to see how easily you can find your product or service for free with a quick search online.

Are people likely to pay for bananas if you can get free bananas in the local banana directory? Probably not, so cross out anything that's not directly saleable.

You'll also want to check that your list is feasible and profitable.

There's no point selling bananas if you can't get hold of bananas to sell, or if it costs more to buy the bananas than you can easily sell them for, so cross off anything that's not financially viable.

Your list should now be short and sweet. You may find that you only have one or two items left – this is a good thing!

When you have just one thing remaining on your list, you've found your business superpower. Your business superpower is the thing you do for dream clients (your best solution) that is both fulfilling to you and helpful to the people you serve. It's a high-value solution that people are willing to pay good money for.

In the coming chapters, we will identify and reverse-engineer your dream client with reference to this business superpower.

Going back to our bridge analogy, when the dream client moves from their land of darkness and confusion, across your brand-story bridge, to your island of light and joy, they will be willing to buy your Ikigai product or service, and they will want your business superpower.

You must be clear about what that business superpower is before you reverse-engineer the client who wants it into your business design.

A QUICK EXERCISE

Before you continue with the next chapter, take a moment to complete this exercise for your business. For each product or service in your Ikigai list, complete the following prompts:

- I am good at this because:

- People need this because:

- People will be willing to pay for this because:

For example, if you're a graphic designer and your business superpower is logo design, you may write:

- I am good at logos because I'm good at illustration.

- People need logos because images are a universal language.

- People will be willing to pay for logos because having a good logo can make a business instantly recognisable.

Keep your answers brief and to the point. Just a single sentence is enough for each. Repeat the exercise for every product and service on your Ikigai list. If you feel you need to remove some products or services from the list once you've done the exercise, then do.

Be ruthless about making this list as short as possible, and ideally, try to limit your list to just two or three. We don't want a long list, we want a powerful list that sets you up for success.

You may like to have one last look over your list to check that everything on it truly makes you happy, because for the rest of this book, we will use your Ikigai list to reverse-engineer the people who want only what's on this list – and nothing more – into your business.

Learning to say no is a difficult milestone in business. It may feel a little scary to ignore or eliminate many of your existing services, especially if you've been in business for a long time and view these tedious parts of your business as your bread-and-butter revenue. Try to wean them out as soon as you feasibly can, as long as you can afford to let them go. Obviously, if you need the sale to eat, then eat, but if you can afford to risk losing a client for the sake of the greater good, then narrowing down your products and services will set you up to design the business you want to have tomorrow.

One of my mentors asked a brilliant question recently. She said, "Do you have the courage to let go of something that's previously worked well for you?"

Letting go of a comfort zone is never easy, especially when we think something is working. The key is to trust the process.

If you keep holding on to the things that hold you back, you'll continue to feel stuck. If you keep chasing bad leads, you'll just waste countless hours explaining what you do to the wrong types of people who will never *properly* understand what you do.

But when you start with the end in mind and place your Ikigai services at the heart of the client's success story, then you can put your dream clients first and reverse-engineer high-value people into your business ecosystem with effortless ease.

This process of figuring out your business superpower from the outset allows you to sell with care by providing the right care to your clients, while also being very selective about who you invite onto your island of light and joy.

If you trust the process, and if you do the hard work now, then you'll get to sell your services to people who come to you, because they recognise you can help them, and they want *you* to solve their underlying need for them.

Regardless of your target prospect's current awareness level, this process of refining your business superpower by eliminating everything that detracts from the business you want guarantees that every person you work with is always a version of your dream client, because every person you work with is always getting a version of the best solution you can offer.

Key takeaways

If you keep holding on to the things that hold you back, you'll continue to accidentally design the wrong types of leads into your business ecosystem.

Refine your list of preferred products and services to find your Ikigai – your reason for being as a business. These Ikigai products and services should be the shortest possible list of the things you really excel at – your business superpowers!

- What are you good at?

- What do you enjoy?
- What do people need?

- What are people willing to pay for?

The products and services you decide on at this stage of the process should represent the business you want tomorrow.

Going back to our island analogy, when the dream client arrives on your island of light and joy, these are the products and services you'll want them to buy from you.

When you start with the end in mind and place your business superpower at the heart of the client's success story, then you can work out who your dream client should be. This lets you put your dream clients first to reverse-engineer high-value people into your business ecosystem with effortless ease.

Remember, everything that detracts from your preferred products and services will ultimately cause you to fill your business with the wrong types of people.

Don't say yes to everything. Learn to say no by slashing your non-Ikigai products or services, so you can focus only on those products and services that can bring both money and joy into your business.

Make sure you're happy with your (very short) list of Ikigai products and services before moving on to the next section, because we'll develop your brand story for the client who wants your business superpower, and only your business superpower.

Be ruthless about saying no to everything that doesn't naturally set you up for lasting success!

CHAPTER 5

WHO CARES?

'You can't transform something you don't understand.'- Annette Franz, founder of CX Journey Inc.

By this stage of the process you should have a clear idea of the common problem that your target clients face. You'll have a (very) short list of Ikigai products or services that define your business superpower.

You'll also be crystal-clear on what you want people to buy from you when they cross your brand-story bridge from their land of darkness and confusion into your carefully designed business ecosystem – the island of light and joy, where all their needs are met, and all their problems can disappear.

We now need to figure out what that dream client looks like.

Who do you care enough about for you to actively want to sell your Ikigai products or services to?

Who would you like to fill your island with, so you can sell yourself to the right people, and only to the right people?

The dream client represents a prototype for the type of person you would like to cross your brand-story bridge, so they can autonomously come to your island and happily buy your stuff from you.

WHO CARES?

One of the biggest challenges business owners face is a lack of people awareness. They don't know who cares enough about their solution to correctly identify their target audience.

Most entrepreneurs do have highly adept people skills, but unfortunately, many of the businesses I've worked with have come to me feeling confused. They're unsure about *who* they are trying to speak to, or don't know what to say to people when promoting their business.

How do you know who you want to communicate with when so much of your communication happens via online content that's consumed by busy people who just fit you into their lives on their own terms?

We have no control whatsoever over how our content is read.

Sure, when you sit down and write your website, your sales proposals, your emails, your social media content, or any other marketing communications you choose to use, the dream scenario is that somebody will relax in a quiet space and give it their full, undivided attention for as long as you'd like them to.

Dreams are free, but life just doesn't work like that.

People who read your content will consume it while they're doing other things. Maybe they'll open your website on a bus, or flick through a few pages of your book while running their evening bath. Some people may glance at your messages when the TV divides their attention, and others will simply scroll past you with 25 other thoughts in their minds.

Attention is the world's most valuable commodity, and we have little to no control over the attention of others. So, who do you speak to when you have just one shot at being heard above the noise, and only one opportunity to say the right thing?

Who cares about what you can really do for them?

If you've ever spent a few minutes with a talkative child of the questioning age, you'll know how the 'but why?' game works. Conversations in the 'but why?' game look a bit like this:

> Inquisitive child: 'Why do fish live in water?'
> Bored adult: 'Because fish like water.'
> Inquisitive child: 'But why do fish live in water?'
> Bored adult: 'Because fish need water to breathe.'
> Inquisitive child: 'Why do fish need water to breathe?'
> Bored adult: 'Because fish have gills instead of lungs.'
> Inquisitive child: 'Why do fish have gills?'
> Bored adult: 'Because fish can't breathe on land.'

This game can go on all day if you let it, particularly if you're on a long car journey. It's a valuable game. As we see here, the child asks, 'Why do fish live in water?' and the adult finally answers, 'Because fish can't breathe on land.'

It takes a few rounds to get there. The bored adult's first answer might start with something closer to, 'Because they like it,' to which an inquisitive child will surely respond with, 'But why do they like it?'

The chances of a bored adult producing an insightful answer like, 'Because fish can't breathe on land' to a child's first question, 'Why do fish live in water?' is close to zero.

Ideas and prototypes need to be worked and reworked until they fall into place just the way they should. You can play the game all day. The longer it goes on for, the better the answers become, even if the bored adult thinks the inquisitive child is getting a little tedious.

This lesson in basic childlike curiosity is one of the most valuable games you can play with your business. Instead of asking 'but why,' just ask 'who cares?'

Instead of getting hung up on creating all sorts of hypothetical audience personas, or 'avatars' as the marketing world likes to call them, it's better to interrogate your idea of what the right audience might look like with a series of who-cares questions.

Who do you want to fill your island with?

For the next few chapters I'll use a fictional business as an example to show you the process in action. I'm going to pick a travel agent because the travel industry is part of a collection of industries that are known for being massively complex with high competition, but it actually doesn't really matter what your business does – the process is the same.

Similar complexities exist in everything from coaching services to SaaS, scented candles, and streamlined professional services. What you do in your business makes no difference at all to the process we'll use.

You can apply the same methodology to any business in any industry – just think about the details for your own business as we go through the principles of Enriched Marketing.

Thinking about our fictional travel agent example, we can say that travel agents can do anything from booking hotels to transfers, tours, trains, and flights for travel to any destination in the world. They can arrange any standard of travel from backpacking with a dome tent to staying in the world's most exclusive resorts. Some travel agents also assist with visas and concierge services, and many will write travel-related content to educate people through information products.

If we try to do everything for everybody, as many people in these industries frequently do, then we end up with the 'always-say-yes' issue where we keep taking on something new but never really develop anything clear in our service list.

These industries are all known for their choice-of-service complexity, so choosing an Ikigai service is essential to success. Coming back to our travel agent example, let's assume that our travel agent has selected 'booking luxury hotels' as their Ikigai service.

Booking luxury hotels is niche – not everybody chooses a hotel, and those that do choose hotels (over, say, campervans) don't always choose luxury hotels.

Now, if the travel agent just uses conventional thinking to choose a target market, they might assume that people who like luxury hotels are rich people who are used to getting spoiled. Rich people who like all the luxury trimmings are a common target audience in the travel industry because it's easy to assume that rich people like to live in the lap of luxury.

Many rich people do like to feel spoiled in luxury hotels, but this is not always true.

If we don't interrogate the idea, it becomes too easy to create a business around lavish or spoiled rich people who like luxury things, without any real insight into who the ideal client really is. This business will surely fail, because the target audience is not correct, and the business owner has no idea who they're trying to speak to in a crowded market.

Tapping into childlike curiosity changes the game. A better approach is to start the dream client interrogation by asking a series of who-cares questions. Our travel agent may start asking questions like this:

- I book luxury hotels. Who cares about staying at luxury hotels?

- People who like nice things. Who cares about nice things?

- People who feel like they deserve nice things. Who cares about that?

- People who work hard for their money. Who cares about hard work?

- Ambitious people. Who cares about ambition?

- People who value opportunities. So, who cares about opportunity?

- People who are driven to succeed. Who cares about success?

- Workaholics. Who cares about being a workaholic?

- People who like to be busy. Who cares about staying busy?

- People who struggle to take proper breaks.

From this short exercise, we can now say that our travel agent books luxury hotels for ambitious people who struggle to take proper breaks. That's a very different target market to rich people who are used to being spoiled.

WRITE YOUR MISSION STATEMENT

We can now use this insightful information to understand what the business really does. We'll work backwards through our thought process to produce a mission statement for the business.

A mission statement is a short, succinct summary of what you do and who you do it for. It sums up what people can expect when they come from their land of darkness and confusion to your island of light and joy.

There's an easy template, which looks like this:

I help (who) to (do what) through (which Ikigai product or service).

In the travel agent example above, this business might use the mission statement template to say:

'I help ambitious people to take proper breaks through booking luxury hotels.'

Notice how the mission statement doesn't speak about the actual service beyond defining what the service does. This business books luxury hotels, so the mission statement focuses on who the service helps, and who cares about having the service.

Other businesses may have mission statements which look similar to this:

'I help innovative entrepreneurs to attract dream clients through reverse-engineered brand stories.'

'I help stressed divorcees to regain their confidence through mindful yoga.'

Your mission statement is informed by your Ikigai service, and refined by those who care about getting your Ikigai service.

Just like Apple only speaks to people who believe they can change the world, we have largely eliminated the features from your message to focus only on the human story.

'Mindful yoga' speaks about the experience of doing yoga. We don't need to say that it's 38-degree Bikram yoga with 26 purpose-driven postures to show the benefit of coming to class.

Notice too how we have defined the essence of the business without listing a single feature. We don't say that you book the best-located hotels, or that you have the cheapest rates or the most experienced staff. We don't say you have won awards or that your team has over 100 years of collective experience.

None of these things matter to the dream client, because

the client just wants a proper break with a quality experience. For that, they need someone who can book them into a luxury hotel. They're thinking about themselves, not about you.

It doesn't matter if you're the best, fastest, most streamlined, most technologically advanced luxury-hotel-booking travel agent on the planet. The only thing that matters is what you do, who you help, and why they care about getting your help.

With that mentality, how you relate to your competition is largely irrelevant too, because USPs and competitor analysis are about you and your competitors, when really, everything you do should be about your customers.

If you put yourself and your business objectives first, then you'll build a reactive business that serves you first. This sets you up to fail. But, if you put your dream client at the heart of your mission statement, then you'll always have the client in the foreground of your brand's purpose, which attracts dream clients and lets you easily win the business off your competition every single time.

Everything you do in Enriched Marketing needs to be about them, the customers, not you, the business.

Nailing down your core service and the people you want to sell it to sets the path for reverse-engineering your dream client into your business design. This exercise defines what the ideal business design looks like. The simpler the service, the better the outcome. If you need to narrow down your Ikigai services again, do that now, then do it again, until you have one resounding service that solves one specific problem.

Our next task is to take a deep dive into the psychology of ambitious people who value quality experiences, and don't get enough time to take a proper break.

A QUICK EXERCISE

Go through your Ikigai service list and cross off anything that now seems irrelevant to your refined business design. Choose your strongest, most valuable service, and run it through a who-cares interrogation to define your dream client.

Complete these two sentences:

- My core service is:

- Who really cares about this is:

(For the second sentence, start with the last answer in your who-cares questions, then bring in any other elements that you think help to really define your dream client – though remember to keep this short and simple.)

Write your business mission statement following the same format as the example for our travel agent.

I help (who) to (do what) through (which Ikigai product or service).

Once this is done, you're ready to delve deep into the hearts and minds of the people who care, so you can reverse-engineer them into your ideal brand story.

WHY DOES IT MATTER?

Now that you have your mission statement tied to the right type of client, and you know how you want to help that client, we need to unwrap why that matters to the client.

Why do they care about it?

In the travel agent example, we used a series of who-cares questions to refine the type of person that cares about staying in luxury hotels. We discovered that for this business, the people who care most about the service offered are ambitious people who struggle to take proper breaks.

We want to find out why that's a problem, and why solving it matters. This will help us draw out the dream client's underlying psychology in the next section.

The process is the same. Write down your mission statement and interrogate your statement with, 'So, why?'

For our travel agent, the answers may look a bit like this:

'I help ambitious people to take proper breaks through booking luxury hotels.'

So why do ambitious people struggle to take proper breaks? Because they don't know when to stop working.

Why don't they know when to stop working? Because they like to be in control of their business.

Why do they like to be in control of their business? Because they want to have an impact on their industry.

Why do they want to have an impact on their industry? Because they want to feel recognised for what they can do.

Why do they want to feel recognised? Because they've put a lot of time and effort into mastering their craft.

Why have they put time and effort into mastering their craft? Because they want to achieve financial freedom.

Why do they want to achieve financial freedom? So they can enjoy life's simple pleasures on their own terms.

From this exercise, we can see that our clients care about taking proper breaks because they want to enjoy life's simple pleasures. We can also see that they need a proper break because they care about mastery, and this means they work too hard to allow themselves proper breaks.

Keep going until you feel something click into place. When you land on the right reason why, you'll know that it's right instinctively because it will align with your Ikigai in your own mind.

KEY TAKEAWAYS

In Enriched Marketing, your business design needs to be about them, the customers, not you, the business.

Instead of highlighting your many USPs to stand out from your competition, it's better to highlight the type of person you want to sell your best Ikigai service to.

Use a childlike curiosity to interrogate your target market for your most valuable product or service. Your goal is to figure out who really cares about whatever it is you want to do.

At the end of the who-cares questions, you should have a crystal-clear understanding of who you want to fill your island of light and joy with. Write your mission statement for this person using the formula.

I help (who) to (do what) through (which Ikigai product or service).

Once you have your mission statement, interrogate it with a series of why questions to find out why your Ikigai service matters to the people who care about whatever it is your business does.

For the next few chapters, we'll delve deeply into the psychological and emotional triggers that can ignite the yes response in this ideal person who cares about whatever it is you do, and will become your dream client.

Make sure you're happy with who your dream client is because you're going to get to know them incredibly well! This is the person we will reverse-engineer into your brand story, so you can attract the right types of people into your business and grow your profits the easy way.

SECTION 2

EXPLORING THE DREAM CLIENT'S DEEP PSYCHOLOGY

CHAPTER 6

THE MONKEY, THE REPTILE, AND THE EVERYDAY JACKASS!

'Neuroscience research shows that very few psychological problems are the result of defects in understanding; most originate in pressures from deeper regions in the brain that drive our perception and attention.' - Bessel van der Kolk, leading psychiatrist

Before we continue with this section, I would like to address an elephant in the room. Neuroscientists, philosophers, and psychologists have been arguing since time began, but they all agree on one thing – the physical brain and the human mind are very different things that just don't mix.

Neuroscientists study the physical brain. Psychologists look at the mind, and philosophers create theories to help us understand complex subjects like, 'What goes on inside the human head?'

Since this is a sales book and our goal is to create a sales philosophy that persuades people to buy from you, I've taken some liberties and have drawn inspiration from early neuroscience, psychology, and studies of inherent motivation to form a sales philosophy around the monkey, the reptile, and the everyday jackass.

These elements work well together in sales and marketing, so within the context of this book and my sales philosophy, when I refer to the brain, the deep psychology, or the human mind, what I'm referring to is 'the inner workings of your dream client' or 'what goes on inside their heads when they choose to buy from you'.

Many books have been written on psychology, sales techniques and brand storytelling which have collectively influenced my approach to creating Enriched Marketing. These teachings, together with my own life experiences gained living and working on five different continents, have shaped my approach to sales and marketing.

There is a list of recommended reading at the end of this book, where you can find deeper research into the core topics discussed here. What you'll learn here is my own interpretation of how an enormous amount of widely published research about the human mind fits together from a sales perspective.

Let's start with taking a whirlwind tour of the inside of the human head.

Scientists have understood for some time that we all have three important areas in our brains, which is an early model of thinking known as the triune brain theory.

Triune brain theory was put forward by renowned neuroscientist, Paul MacLean, in the 1960s. It suggests that our brains have three basic components, which together make up the brain's physiological, cognitive, and emotional capacity.

The first part of the brain in triune brain theory is the reptilian brain. When the reptilian brain recognises a threat, we feel compelled to act a certain way to keep us safe. It is widely accepted that we react in these situations with a fight, flight, freeze response. This part of the brain is where the brain stem is found, and its job is to keep us alive.

The second part of the brain is the mammalian brain, which is responsible for the limbic system. This part of the brain controls our emotions and is where we find the amygdala.

The third part of the brain is the neocortex, which is where our conscious thought processes happen. Here, we use our higher thinking skills for things like speech and logic. This is where we do our active thinking, and this part of the brain is the only part that we're directly aware of in our daily living.

While we are physically alive and do feel emotions, the workings of the reptilian and mammalian brains are hidden in the unconscious and subconscious minds. We're unaware of them. We can't just press a little button that switches us into mammalian mode, in the same way that Buzz Lightyear was switched into Spanish mode in *Toy Story 3* – as nice as that would be sometimes!

Triune brain theory originally hypothesised that each of our three brains has a unique job to do, with no overlap, but this has since been significantly developed in the fast-paced world of science.

Today, it's largely understood that the various parts of our brains can sometimes work together, and are not always independent of each other.

In psychology, which studies the mind, it's accepted that we have three layers of thinking, which are known as conscious thought, subconscious thought, and unconscious thought.

Likewise, in the field of philosophy, we see theories which describe humans as having mind, body, and soul.

Despite the ongoing arguments about mind–body dualism and the clear distinctions between physical neuroscience and the studies of the mind in psychology, we can use these three parallel views to say that we have three clear layers inside our heads.

We have the stem brain, the unconscious mind, and the soul, which keep us alive and make us who we are. In the middle layer, we have the amygdala, the subconscious mind, and the heart, which help us to feel and to understand our emotions. Finally, we have the neocortex, the conscious mind, and the head, which is where we experience daily living.

Using these parallel fields of study for inspiration means we can now create a sales-specific framework – the 'sales brain' – that maps how your dream clients make decisions about your business with predictable results.

In the sales brain, our three 'brains' have decision-making jobs to do that can influence whether or not somebody says yes to your offer.

I like to call the three sales-brain layers the reptile, the monkey, and the everyday jackass, or the reptilian brain, the everyday brain, and the monkey brain.

THE FIRST LAYER IN SALES IS THE REPTILIAN BRAIN.

This is the unconscious mind that's responsible for keeping us safe and well. Inside this part of the mind and brain is a system of deep psychological and physiological needs that we're largely unaware of.

When the reptile feels scared or uncomfortable, it has the capacity to influence how we behave. This is why we have the fight, flight, or freeze reflex when we feel threatened or scared, and why we do things unconsciously in certain situations.

The reptile is responsible for helping us feel both emotionally and psychologically safe, so it's here in the client's deepest psychology that we can find what really motivates people at a core level.

We can say that the reptile represents the soul. It's motivated by who we really are in our deepest layer. In sales, our reptilian brain is where we are hardwired to respond in predictable ways to specific situations. It's what makes us need the things you sell.

THE SECOND LAYER IN SALES IS THE EVERYDAY JACKASS.

This is the conscious part of the mind that's responsible for maintaining rational thought, exploring the imagination, and making key decisions in our everyday lives.

We know what goes on in our conscious thoughts because

this is where we do our daily living. We can learn to control our thoughts relatively easily in the conscious mind, even when we don't want to. We see this in the formation of new habits. It's possible to train yourself to stop eating chocolate, even when you don't particularly want to do that.

Unfortunately, this part of the mind can sometimes consciously choose not to give us what we want or need, even when it knows better.

You may find that you need a break, but your rational side tells you to keep working. Maybe you've injured yourself and you know you need to give your body time to recover, but you go for that run anyway, even if it hurts. You might really want to try something new, but you rationalise that you that you shouldn't take the risk.

In storytelling, every good story needs an antagonist, or a conflict. In brand storytelling, the everyday mind is the antagonist – the jackass!

Our minds don't always work in our favour, which is useful in sales, but can sometimes make our inner mental jackass our own biggest enemy. We have the ability to sabotage ourselves because the jackass makes decisions that work against our inner wellness, not for it.

Money is one area where the everyday jackass often trips us up. Perhaps you really want to allow yourself to have something, like meaningful wealth in your business, for example, but your rational brain tells you that you don't deserve it for whatever reason, so you continue to sell yourself short.

The everyday jackass, which represents the head, is present in all of us. It's what sometimes prevents us from getting what we truly want out of life. When this happens, we sometimes say that the heart wants one thing, but the head says another.

THE THIRD LAYER IN SALES IS THE MONKEY BRAIN.

Our monkey brain is responsible for our emotional wellbeing. It thrives on instant gratification, so it's easily distracted, overly energetic, and highly impulsive.

We can say that our monkey brain represents the heart.

The monkey brain often makes rash decisions without much thought for the consequences. It buys holidays you can't comfortably afford, always picks the path of least resistance, and sometimes lets you watch funny videos of cats when you *know* you should be working.

In triune brain theory, the reptilian brain controls what we need, the mammalian brain controls how we feel, and the neocortex controls how we think and behave.

In the sales brain, the everyday jackass controls our daily choices, the monkey controls how we feel, and the reptile controls what we really need to find a sense of purpose.

The Enriched Marketing approach says the everyday jackass makes bad decisions that sabotage the reptile's needs, and the monkey steps in to save the day with an impulse buy that makes you feel better, which keeps the reptile happy.

The relationship between the monkey and the everyday

jackass is the relationship between head and heart. When they agree, we find inner peace and the reptile smiles. When they clash, the heart nearly always wins in the end.

IN ENRICHED MARKETING, THE MONKEY, THE REPTILE, AND THE EVERYDAY JACKASS SHOULD BE VIEWED AS A SMALL PURCHASING TEAM THAT WILL ULTIMATELY BUY YOUR PRODUCTS AND SERVICES.

The reptile's job is to make sure we're getting what we need to survive and thrive, both physiologically and psychologically. The everyday jackass is tasked with making good, rational decisions. And the monkey brain creates powerful emotions that allow us to have some instant gratification when we start feeling bad or taking ourselves too seriously.

Despite our natural complexity, humans are actually very easy to influence if you understand how these three characters fit together in the consumer decision-making process.

Our inner reptile has a deep psychological need that we spend our entire lives trying to meet, such as the need for independence, social connection, recognition, or control. Studies in self-determination theory* conducted by Edward Deci and

---

* Deci, E.L. and Ryan, R.M. (1985) 'Conceptualizations of intrinsic motivation and self-determination' in *Intrinsic Motivation and Self-Determination in Human Behavior: Perspectives in Social Psychology*. Boston, MA: Springer.

Richard Ryan show we choose to behave according to our intrinsic motivators because fulfilling our psychological needs is inherently rewarding.

We get a greater kick out of meeting this need than we do from the actual task. Recognition for achieving a goal is oftentimes more rewarding than the project itself. Staying in control of a situation can be more rewarding than the outcome.

This is commonly seen in things like dieting. People who diet feel good because they gain control over their weight, achieve a personal goal, boost their confidence in social settings, or become more connected to others through improved self-esteem. We stay motivated to stick to a diet because the psychological benefits of losing weight feel good, not because we want to eat diet meals.

If a person is intrinsically motivated by a deep psychological need for structure and order, they will consistently seek out the reward of feeling in control. They can't ignore the desire for control because the reptilian brain decides what it needs, and that core need is formed in the unconscious mind where we can't easily access or control it.

When our core need isn't properly met, we produce negative emotions which affect our conscious thinking. We say things like, 'I'm not getting what I need,' or, 'This makes me uncomfortable.'

The discomfort experienced when the reptile's deep psychological need is not being met causes the monkey brain to overcompensate with impulsive purchases that meet that need. This facilitates the production of happy feelings that make the discomfort go away.

For example, if a person who needs independence is feeling

trapped in their job or their long-term relationship, they may book an impulsive holiday, cheat on their spouse, or call in sick to avoid feeling uncomfortable at work.

This is a rash decision that's fundamentally motivated by an underlying psychological need that's not being met at a deeper level. The everyday jackass is not giving the reptile enough freedom, so the monkey solves the problem with some instant gratification.

Many people will spend a fair amount of time and money on therapy trying to learn how they can change themselves to make peace with an uncomfortable situation that doesn't meet their needs. They look for ways to befriend an everyday jackass that continues to sabotage them, but they don't let the monkey out of its cage, and they don't allow their reptile to get what it wants.

As many good psychologists will tell you, at the end of any journey of self-discovery the best outcome is to reach a place of acceptance, where people can make peace with who they are and feel their feelings, instead of just fighting against themselves to make do with something that isn't psychologically healthy for them.

For example, the person who needs independence may struggle with a relationship that squashes their sense of freedom. This can cause a range of difficult emotions to surface like self-doubt, low self-esteem, and anger. If the everyday jackass drives their life, they stay in the bad relationship and the monkey creates negative feelings, which the jackass often tries to ignore.

When a state of self-realisation is achieved, the person will learn to accept their need for independence. They start to recognise how the monkey is feeling, and they take steps to ensure the jackass makes better decisions.

In therapy, this will often result in the everyday jackass ending the bad relationship to facilitate the freedom they need, which allows the monkey brain to create happy emotions again.

During my years working on cruise ships, I got to experience the intensity of life in a pressure can. Cruise crew come from all walks of life, and nearly all of them have some sort of challenge they're running from. Everybody lives in close quarters, working 8–10 months at a time, 12–16 hours a day, 7 days a week with no days off.

There's a camaraderie and a closeness that exists between people who would otherwise never get to interact. In my teams, I frequently had one person from each continent, or five people called five variations of 'Michael' in five different languages.

I learned to observe, and to seek understanding of the human condition through my daily interactions. Sometimes, a person who had been living in the slums of Delhi would manage people from the hills of Bel Air. Sometimes, people from war-torn countries would be required to work in the same team and share a 6ft cabin with no window.

There's a running joke in the cruise industry: crew are either running from something or looking for something.

What I observed is that people are by and large all looking for the same things. They want to feel independent, motivated to achieve something, connected to friends and family, or inspired to take control of their lives.

Understanding this is the cornerstone of successful selling, because it shows how buyers are motivated beyond the things they choose to buy.

RECOGNISE THAT THE MONKEY AND THE REPTILE ARE BEST FRIENDS.

If the reptilian brain is happy, the everyday brain can focus on living a good life, and the monkey brain stops rebelling against the everyday brain with impulsive decisions that bring instant gratification.

This is a very comfortable state of homeostasis for consumers, and they will gladly give you their money if you can help them maintain this level of psychological balance. It equates to happiness and fulfilment, which as it turns out, can be bought.

The monkey brain gets a lot of bad rep, because this is where distraction and procrastination thrive. Left unchecked, the monkey brain can spend hours scrolling through online stores making impulsive purchases that the everyday brain wouldn't dream of making.

But this is a good thing for both sellers and consumers.

The monkey brain is responsible for making sure that the reptilian brain gets what it needs, because our everyday jackass brain that's filled with too much rational thought can't always be trusted to get that right.

In brand storytelling, rational decision-making is the antagonist. The monkey's job is to recognise when the everyday brain is making bad – but rational – decisions that don't align properly with the reptile's needs. When it sees a red flag, it acts impulsively until the everyday brain notices and takes steps to rectify the situation, which in the eyes of the jackass stops the monkey's bad behaviour, but in the eyes of the reptile creates a state of desirable homeostasis.

For example, if the reptilian brain needs independence and the everyday brain chooses a relationship that squashes freedom, then the monkey brain will either cause bad behaviour in that relationship until the relationship ends, or it will purchase some therapy to achieve the same result.

To stop the monkey from taking over, the everyday brain must learn to accept what the reptilian brain needs and give it what it's asking for – independence. The monkey will always advocate for the reptile, so the monkey buys things for the reptile, and the jackass is forced to agree.

In Enriched Marketing, we use this inherent part of human nature to our advantage to sell effortlessly to the people who we can best help with our Ikigai service.

It's a very simple process that works like this:

Step 1 – Find out what the dream client's reptilian brain needs at a core level

Carl Jung, the founder of analytical psychology, theorised that our core psychological need comes from a desire for independence, control, social belonging, or recognition.

In our relationship example, the reptilian brain needs independence. In someone who struggles to collaborate with others, that may be control.

STEP 2 – HIGHLIGHT HOW THE DREAM CLIENT'S EVERYDAY BRAIN IS FAILING TO MEET THE REPTILE'S NEED

How is the customer's problem working against their ability to achieve their deepest desire?

In our relationship example, the customer's relationship (which was chosen by the everyday jackass) is causing the client to feel trapped. What is your dream client struggling with?

STEP 3 – SHOW THE MONKEY BRAIN AN INSTANT-GRATIFICATION, SHINY SOLUTION THAT FILLS THE DREAM CLIENT'S CORE NEED

In our relationship example, the instant gratification is therapy which, over time, can help the everyday brain understand how to end the relationship, thereby achieving the desired independence.

In a different example, a person may be motivated by social connection.

If you're selling tickets to an event, you might highlight that not being part of the event will cause people to feel left out.

The customer's monkey instantly recognises that feeling left out equates to social isolation, so it buys the ticket to social connection before the jackass has time to say no.

The same process can be applied to absolutely anything, as long as you're always acting in the customer's best interest. Your solution must be genuinely helpful, and they must be experiencing authentic pain that's caused by the problem you solve.

In our therapy example, the trapped person feels the pain of entrapment, and therapy is genuinely helpful for regaining independence. For our event seller, the isolated person feels the pain of loneliness, and the ticket bought is a helpful way to feel connected to others.

Let's go back to our travel agent's mission statement for a moment.

Using a series of 'who cares' questions, we wrote the following mission statement for our travel agent: 'I help ambitious people to take proper breaks through booking luxury hotels.'

How does the three-brained approach apply to the ambitious people we wish to sell to in this example?

We can say that ambitious people commonly have high-flying jobs or run their own businesses. This is oftentimes because they struggle to fit into the confines of a managed day job where they're told what to do and how to do it. They frequently prefer to think for themselves and to follow their own visions.

From this general observation, it can be assumed that many of the travel agent's targeted ambitious people will have a deep-seated need for independence. With that in mind, we can trigger a sense of entrapment by highlighting that our targeted ambitious people are working so hard that they're not getting enough free time in their jobs to take proper breaks.

At the same time, we can present their monkey brains with an instant-gratification opportunity to book a quality experience at a luxury hotel.

An impulsive purchase decision can be made by the monkey brain, whose sole job is to make sure that the ambitious person's deep need for independence is met.

The everyday brain that's trapped in a cycle of working too hard with too little time off will eventually get outnumbered by the monkey and the reptilian brains, and this person will have no choice but to give them what they need – a break and a nice hotel, where they can escape from the pressures of working too hard.

This person will book a luxury hotel without bothering about the travel agent's USPs, because the monkey has chosen something that fundamentally keeps the reptile happy, and the reptile always wins.

Over the next few chapters, we'll look at these concepts in greater detail when we delve into Carl Jung's archetypes.

Let's jump right in!

Key takeaways

It's largely accepted amongst psychologists that people have three layers of thinking. Further reading is widely available on this, but a good source of information is *The Body Keeps the Score* by Bessel van der Kolk.

- **The reptilian brain** is our unconscious mind, which is responsible for keeping us safe.

- **The everyday brain** is our conscious mind, responsible for daily living and rational thought.

- **The monkey brain** is our impulsive decision-making brain, responsible for keeping the everyday brain aligned with the reptilian brain.

The reptilian brain has deep psychological needs, and will always try to fill these needs. When the everyday brain makes rational decisions that don't fill the reptilian brain's core needs, then the monkey intervenes. The monkey brain can overrule the everyday brain, and will always do what the reptilian brain needs.

People who feel conflicted in decision-making are often torn between their head and their heart. The heart wants one thing, and the head wants another. In situations like this, the heart nearly always wins in the long run. The heart represents what the reptilian brain wants, and the head represents what the everyday brain thinks it wants.

We can use this information to inspire impulsive decisions. To achieve this, all we need to do is highlight how the customer's problem is failing to meet their deep psychological need, then give the monkey something to buy that does meet this need.

The money and the reptile are best friends, so the monkey will always do what the reptile needs to thrive. If you want to attract people who want to buy from you, the best way to do that is to work out what the dream client needs in their deep psychology.

People throughout the world spend time and money in therapy trying to understand why they are unhappy. In 2023, the global psychology and counselling market is estimated to be just over $53 billion. Nearly always, the outcome of psychological therapy is to reach a place where the client's inherent psychological needs are accepted, not resisted.

This elevated self-awareness helps people to change their thought patterns in the everyday brain to advocate for their deeper reptilian needs, which calms the monkey brain, and keeps the reptile happy.

Sales and psychology are very closely linked. The techniques you'll learn here to harness the power of deep psychology in sales should always be used responsibly. It's important to make ethical decisions that always and only act in the dream client's best interests, so you can genuinely help them to meet their needs in a safe environment.

Sell with care!

CHAPTER 7

CARL JUNG AND THE TWELVE ARCHETYPES

'In all chaos there is a cosmos, in all disorder a secret order.' - Carl Jung, father of modern psychology

O n 26 July 1875, the world was graced with the birth of Carl Gustav Jung, a Swiss psychiatrist who later became known as 'the father of analytical psychology'. Carl Jung's theories are broad and deep, but they embrace a very simple idea:

People share a collective unconscious. Within the scope of what makes us human, we can be grouped according to basic archetypes that describe our typical behaviours.

Jung's research into universal patterns and the psychological archetypes analysed the imagery seen in dreams, as well as common symbols that frequently appear in unrelated cultures.

What Carl Jung hypothesised was that similar images were interpreted in similar ways by very different types of people, so he concluded that images and their meanings were therefore universal. If images and symbols share common interpretations across cultures, then there must be a collective unconscious that unites people with a shared underlying psychology.

If people have similar experiences and apply similar themes to things like symbolism, literature, and art – even when they are from vastly different cultures and have no first-hand knowledge of each other – then they must have inherent qualities that make people similar at a core level.

Scientific studies have agreed and argued with Carl Jung and the concept of the collective unconscious since the idea was born, but that hasn't stopped archetypes from evolving into a user-friendly manual for understanding what motivates people.

Carl Jung's archetype theories have been exciting the world's best brand storytellers for decades, and this is now widely accepted as an effective tool in top-level brand-building.

Although the concept wasn't new at the time, the success of archetype-informed brand storytelling was brought to the forefront in 2001 when Margaret Mark and Carol S. Pearson published a book called *The Hero and The Outlaw: Building Extraordinary Brands Through The Power Of Archetypes*.

I've used archetypes in nearly everything I've written for my clients, with extraordinary results. Clients tell me they feel seen. They report feeling more confident knowing they're achieving their true worth, and they notice significant changes in the clients they attract towards their businesses.

In one such case, a client was struggling with too many clients who have narcissistic personality disorder in a counselling business. This was weighing heavily on their own mental health. A few small tweaks to the sales language used on their website to target a specific archetype, and the client base was completely transformed. The counselling business now attracts people who value empathy and want healthy relationships.

Another client was pitching themselves against a competitor because they felt their competitor's services had a similar quality and style, and that made them my client's biggest rival. We analysed the two businesses alongside each other and found they were not competitors at all. One set of clients was driven by freedom, the other, by control.

In both cases, misaligned brand messaging was causing these businesses to fail by design because they were attracting the wrong types of clients.

Archetype storytelling changed the brand narratives. Changing the stories brought better-quality clients into their business ecosystems, and gave both a powerful competitive edge.

IN BRANDING, AN ARCHETYPE IS A WAY TO DESCRIBE HOW PEOPLE WILL TYPICALLY BEHAVE WHEN PLACED UNDER PRESSURE.

When challenges arise, people will nearly always revert to their inherent human nature, because their psychological profile determines what they really need.

This is the golden thread in Enriched Marketing. If we think of all the world's people as just twelve types of typical behaviours, then we can very easily get to know our ideal person at a deep psychological level.

If human nature has such elegant beauty, then how easy is it to pluck the right emotional strings to gently sway your dream client towards your business? All we need to do is determine which archetype the dream client is, and we can map their reptilian brain's inherent need in great detail.

Better still, if we can build a business that reflects the dream client's inherent psychological need – their reptilian need – then we can become instantly likeable to their monkey brain, and the dream client will come to us to buy whatever it is we're selling.

PERSONALITIES AND ARCHETYPES ARE TWO DIFFERENT THINGS, SO IT'S IMPORTANT TO UNDERSTAND THE DIFFERENCE WHEN BUILDING A BRAND STORY.

Brand archetypes refer to the typical characteristics that we have within a framework of twelve types of behaviours. Our archetype describes what the reptilian brain – our deepest level of unconscious thinking – needs, and what our monkey brain typically looks for to fulfil that need.

Fundamentally, archetypes look at how people inherently respond when placed under pressure. Do they run for the door, look for a supportive friend, take centre stage, or try to control everything in minuscule detail?

The way we behave when we crack under pressure is guided by our archetype. What do we need to feel psychologically safe?

Personalities refer to the qualities that make us individually unique. Are people kind, generous, eccentric, or aloof? Common personality traits exist in equal measure across all archetypes and are not defined by a person's archetype.

Anybody can be kind or aloof, regardless of their archetype, but people of certain archetypes will always be driven by particular sets of behaviours, regardless of their personality traits.

To frame this a different way, our personalities focus on what differentiates us from others, much like our USPs, while our archetype highlights what makes us the same as others.

When marketing to the masses, we need to tap into what lots of individuals who might like to buy our stuff have in common, so that we can write a powerful brand story for many individuals who share a common need for our solution.

In Enriched Marketing, we look at the archetype to understand what people in our pot of dream clients have in common at a deep psychological level. When we know what the dream client's reptilian brain needs to thrive, we can highlight the opposite of that need: the dream client's problem. This inspires the monkey brain in everybody who shares the same psychological profile as the dream client to buy from you.

To attract many clients, we only need to understand one dream client's archetype. Everybody who shares this person's typical response to pressure will relate to the same brand story.

These types of people will come looking for your business, because the monkey and the reptile are best friends, and the reptile always wins.

The only thing that matters to the dream client is whether or not their underlying needs are met. To achieve this, we just need to understand how their archetype affects their decision-making process, so we can trigger the desired response.

So, how do you know what the dream client will do in a pressure pot if you don't know them personally?

CREATE THE DREAM CLIENT'S DEEP PSYCHOLOGICAL PROFILE

Deciding which client archetype to design into your business is intelligent guesswork, and a choice. It's not about figuring out who you have today; it's about working out who you want to work with tomorrow.

You'll use your mission statement and your why reasoning (see Chapter 5) to help you choose the most appropriate archetype. For example, our travel agent helps ambitious people who struggle to take proper breaks, and that matters because these ambitious people want to master their craft for deeper impact, so they can live a simple life without stress.

We'll bear this in mind when choosing an archetype, so think about the people you identified in your mission statement and why your solution matters to your dream client, then make an educated guess on who will be right for your business.

This broad psychological profile defines the type of person you want to bring into your client base, which empowers you to attract everybody who looks like the dream client without trying to create new demand in a pool of mixed-bag people who all have different underlying needs.

Archetype thinking is what lets our travel agent attract people who don't find time for a proper break, regardless of whether or not they're rich or spoiled.

Step 1 – Find the reptile's deep psychological need

The first step is to identify your dream client's core psychological need.

According to Carl Jung's archetype model, there are just twelve typical types of people in total. These twelve typical types of people can be categorised into four subgroups, which define their core psychological need.

The core psychological need in your archetype subgroup describes how people naturally relate to the world around them. Some people want to understand how their world works, while others want to feel in control of their world. Some people want to feel part of their world, while others want to leave a mark on their world.

Within each of the four subgroups, there are three typical

approaches that people who fall into each subgroup will take to meet that core need. This general, typical behaviour is what we call our archetype.

Choosing your future dream client is an intelligent decision that's guided by what you want to achieve tomorrow. We pick the archetype we want to fill our business with, then reverse-engineer the brand story so that it speaks to that type of person, and only to that type of person. This brings top-quality clients towards you, and sends the less-desirable clients to somebody else.

Think about the types of people you like to work with, in general. What do they have in common? Think about your favourite clients who have enabled you to do your best work. What do you like about working with them? Who in your existing ecosystem can best set you up for success?

Using your mission statement and your general life experience as guidance, choose one category from the below subgroups that best fits the type of person you would like to surround yourself with in your client base.

For example, do you like working with people who look at the big picture and find ways to make things easier, or do you prefer working with people who like straight lines and neat little boxes? Would you like to attract clients who want to achieve greatness in life, or do you hope to attract clients who just want to have a good time without too much stress?

Think about the clients you want in the future, remembering that the clients of the future can and may look quite different to the clients you have today.

You might also like to do the exercise for yourself as well as for your dream client.

More often than not, people choose dream clients that are closely aligned to their own archetype, so it's always helpful to consider where you best fit into these categories too.

Complete this sentence: In the successful business that brings me both money and joy, my dream client is driven by their need for:

1. Independence
2. Recognition
3. Social belonging
4. Control

Your choice of subcategory describes the dream client's underlying psychological need, which informs their key decisions.

For our travel agent, whose clients struggle to take proper breaks because they work too hard, we might say that their clients are driven by their need for independence or recognition, but we're less likely to say they are driven by the need for social belonging.

There will be some overlap and you may find you could choose multiple categories. The goal here is to just pick the strongest match, using your best guess. Choose only one, and choose the one you feel is best.

People generally chase this need for all of their lives, and when presented with a choice, will by default choose the option that satisfies this need, whether they want to or not. Research in fields such as learning and development* consistently show

---

* Ryan, R.M. and Deci, E.L. (2009) 'Promoting self-determined school engagement' in Wentzel, K. and Miele, D.B. (eds.) *Handbook of Motivation at School*. Routledge, pp.171–195.

that people who lean into their inherent motivators – their core psychological need – continuously achieve better results than those who don't follow their natural flow.

In real life, we see this in action when people are conflicted by a difficult decision. They may say, 'My head wants one thing, but my heart wants another.' This happens because the everyday brain, the head, is trying to choose something that works against the reptilian brain's core need, the heart.

Nearly always, the heart wins. When the heart doesn't win, then nearly always, the monkey brain intervenes and rebels against the everyday brain's logical decision with an impulse purchase that meets the reptile's need. In the end, the reptilian brain always wins.

If you know what this core need is in your preferred dream client, then all you need do to entice their yes response is highlight how this need is unfulfilled in their current problem, and satisfy it with your service.

Remember, when choosing your archetype subcategory, you just want to choose the type of person that can best set you up for success. Do you like working with people who want to leave an impact, feel in control, build relationships, or chase their independence?

Choose the typical type of person you want to fill your business with tomorrow, even if the kinds of people you attract today are very different. Most people will have some element of all of these needs. You only want to choose one subcategory, so if your dream client can fit into two or more subcategories, then just pick the strongest one.

STEP 2 – FIND THE MONKEY BRAIN'S GUILTY PLEASURE

Within each of these four subcategories, people will typically fill their underlying psychological need for independence, recognition, social belonging, or control using a slightly different approach.

This is the approach that people can't help but like. It's the monkey's guilty pleasure, or the scenario they can't resist. When placed under pressure, people will resort to this comfort zone to get themselves out of an uncomfortable situation.

Now that we know which of the four subcategories your preferred client's reptilian brain best fits into, let's look at how they achieve that deep psychological need by exploring what makes their monkey brain happy.

Each of the four subcategories have three variations, which together make up Carl Jung's twelve archetypes.

GROUP 1: THE DESIRE FOR INDEPENDENCE

The reptilian need for independence is resolved when people find freedom. Dream clients who have a fundamental need for independence are on a quest to reach a better life.

People who desire independence genuinely believe that the grass really is greener on the other side, so they seek out experiences that enable them to free themselves from whatever is holding them back.

Archetype: INNOCENT

Innocent people gain independence through developing their inner peace and happiness. This archetype treasures life's simplest pleasures, and feels free when they're comfortable with who they are.

They value purity of heart, and want to feel safe. The opposite of this is insecurity. Innocent monkey brains can be triggered to regain a sense of safety when the everyday brain feels insecure.

Archetype: EXPLORER

Explorers find independence by exploring their outer world. They're always on an adventure, and they never say no to trying new things if it means they can discover what the grass is like over there.

These types of people value escapism, and want to feel the wind in their hair. Explorer monkey brains can be triggered by feeling fenced in, which will cause them to want to get out of their situation at any cost.

Archetype: SAGE

Sage looks for independence by using knowledge as a guide. They're continually learning how things work, and when placed under pressure, will intellectualise their way to a better place.

They value understanding, and want to feel competent. Sage monkey brains can be triggered by confusion, so keeping them in the dark or showing gaps in their knowledge will cause them to crave answers.

GROUP 2: THE DESIRE FOR RECOGNITION

Dream clients in this group want to leave their mark on the world. Their burning desire is to have an impact on others, good or bad. People who desire recognition want to create impact. This group wants to be remembered for doing something great that sets them apart.

ARCHETYPE: HERO

Heroes look for recognition by mastering their skills. They want to be the very best. They push themselves to achieve the pinnacle of high performance, and they never settle for anything less.

They value quality, and want to feel accomplished. They're disciplined, and like to feel strong.

Hero monkey brains can be triggered by failure. If they feel like they're not reaching their full potential, they will push themselves to the brink to become the best. Ultimately, the heroes compete with themselves, and never give up.

Archetype: MAGICIAN

Magicians look for recognition by chasing power. They want to be seen as people who can walk up to solutions and take them effortlessly. They like to empower themselves and others, and want the world to feel like everything and anything is possible.

They value imagination, and want to feel transformative. Magician monkey brains can be triggered by suppression. If they feel like something is made to be impossible, they will find a way to prove you wrong.

Archetype: OUTLAW

Outlaws look for recognition by going against the grain. They want to be seen as a trailblazer, and they're not afraid to be unconventional if it means they can be seen for their inner genius.

They value rebellion, and want to feel free to do whatever they want to do without repercussion. Outlaw monkey brains can be triggered by conformity. When they believe something is boring, they will intentionally stir the pot.

Group 3: The desire for belonging

People who are driven by their need to belong want to feel like they're part of something that's bigger than themselves. They crave social bonding, so look for a sense of community and likeness in others. Where no community exists, people who desire belonging will go out and make a new community with whoever they can find.

Archetype: LOVER

Lovers forge deep, meaningful relationships. They seek pleasure, and thrive on the richness of a life well lived. They desire beauty and romance. Lovers crave sumptuous experiences that can ignite their many senses.

They value meaningful connection, and they want to feel loved. Lover monkey brains can be triggered by injustice. They look for the good in people, so when trust is broken, they will strengthen their social bonds with others.

Archetype: JESTER

Jesters just want to live in the moment and have fun. They're often the life and soul of the party. They're easy to get along with because they desire a world where everybody is having a good time.

They value the simple life, and they want to feel like the big stuff will go away on its own. Jester monkey brains can be triggered by things that are emotionally heavy. They look for ways to avoid difficult topics by using humour as a coping mechanism for overwhelming stress.

Archetype: EVERYMAN

Everyman archetypes are just your regular guy (or girl) next door. They want to fit in and be seen as 'the picture of normal', however that looks to them.

These types of people want to be part of the crowd, and they intentionally don't have strong views on polarising topics. They value how others perceive them, and they want to feel accepted.

Everyman monkey brains can be triggered by social exclusion. They look for common ground with others, so when they feel differentiated, they find ways to present themselves as neutral (like Switzerland).

Group 4: The desire for control

People who are driven by their desire for control want to create order from chaos. They're continually looking for ways to streamline their life experience, and to help others to do the same.

Those with the desire to feel in control crave structure. They work tirelessly to bring systems and processes into everything they touch.

Archetype: RULER

Rulers like things to be measured. These are your classic 'Excel spreadsheet' fanatics who enjoy seeing how small details can impact the big picture. They like things to be as expected because this helps them to compartmentalise their thoughts into manageable parts.

They value predictability, and they like to feel that they have a handle on things. Ruler monkey brains can be triggered by unexpected surprises. They look for ways to understand the future, and like to follow data-driven rules that do what they say on the box.

Archetype: CAREGIVER

Caregivers are motivated by serving others. They want to make life easier for people, so they go out of their way to provide a duty of care that safeguards people's experiences against things which can harm them. Through service, they simplify the lives of others.

They value altruism, and they like to feel that they can make a genuine difference. Caregiver monkey brains can be triggered by seeing others in distress. They will do whatever they can to soothe the situation, so that those affected can feel better.

Archetype: INNOVATOR

Innovators understand that structure determines the outcome. They want to invent creative solutions to complex problems, and recognise that building the right foundations can produce enduring results that provide long-term success.

Innovators value creativity, and want to feel like they're

working towards something important. Innovator brains like taking shortcuts. They will look for flaws in the system, then come up with ingenious ways to plug the gaps for a better tomorrow.

REVERSE-ENGINEERED BRAND STORIES FOR ENRICHED MARKETING ARE BUILT ENTIRELY AROUND THESE PSYCHOLOGICAL PROFILES OF THE IDEAL CLIENT.

If we tell the story that's in people's hearts, they give us their minds.

And their money.

This methodology is used by many of the world's most successful brands because it harnesses a simple human desire for retail therapy. Retail therapy is when we buy something we know we don't need, but are happy about it because it makes us feel good.

When retail therapy does the job of a real therapist, the monkey makes an impulsive purchase and buys a gift for the reptilian brain, which gives the reptile what it needs. The unconscious mind is happy, the impulsive mind slows down, and the everyday brain accepts that the reptile will always win.

In that framework for selling through the power of psychology – where the problem the dream client faces fails to satisfy their deep need, and their impulsive, decision-making monkey brain is offered your solution to satisfy it – it becomes nearly impossible for people to walk away from your service, as long as the solution always has their best interests at heart.

Among the top brands, nearly all of the best sales campaigns use archetype thinking to design the dream client into the business ecosystem. They draw from inherent human nature to activate the existing demand and entice their yes response.

Coca-Cola is a brand of friendship and close connections, so this is a lover archetype. McDonald's invites people to love life's simple moments (the innocent). Apple, the outlaw, has encouraged generations of people to push the human race forward because they're not afraid to be different. Levi, an explorer brand, breathes a sense of freedom into everyday jeans, and TOMS, a caregiver, wins the hearts of altruists by giving away one pair of shoes for every pair purchased.

Archetype thinking allows you to pick and choose who you work with by presenting yourself as a brand that meets the dream client's deepest needs. An easy way to look at this is to think about which flavour clients you want in your business.

If you want chocolate-flavoured clients, all you need to do is make your business feel chocolatey, and chocolate clients will come and find you. If you make your business feel like vanilla, then you'll attract vanilla clients.

So, who do you want to work with when you design your future client base into your brand story?

A QUICK EXERCISE

Think about what your business does (your solution), and who cares about your solution. Choose which of the four archetype subcategories their reptilian brain needs and complete this sentence.

My dream client is driven by a deep need for: (independence, recognition, social belonging, or control).

Now, think about your mission statement within the context of the group you have chosen, and decide how the types of people you like to work with will typically behave to achieve that burning desire. You're making a best-guess, self-informed choice between the three archetypes that fall into your chosen group.

For group one, independence, your target archetype will be an innocent, explorer, or sage. In group two, recognition, the archetype will be a hero, magician, or outlaw. For group three, social belonging, your target archetype will be a lover, jester, or everyman. And for group four, control, the archetype will be a ruler, caregiver, or innovator.

My target dream client's archetype is:

Key takeaways

According to Carl Jung, people can be broadly divided into twelve archetypes, which describe how people will typically behave when placed under pressure.

Archetypes are different to personalities because archetypes describe what many people have in common in their psychological needs, whereas personality traits highlight what makes individuals unique.

The twelve archetypes fit into four groups, which are differentiated by their deepest psychological need: independence, recognition, social belonging, or control.

How we achieve our deepest psychological needs can be slightly different within each category.

- **Independence.** Your dream clients are on a quest to find a state of paradise, wherever that may be. People will follow their inner happiness (innocent), explore their outer worlds (explorer), or intellectualise their experiences (sage).

- **Recognition.** These dream clients want to leave their mark on the world. They achieve this by mastering their craft (hero), chasing power (magician), or rebelling against the ordinary (outlaw).

- **Social belonging.** Dream clients in this group want to build their sense of community. They will seek to form meaningful relationships (lover), live in the moment and encourage others to do the same (jester), or blend in with others (everyman).

- **Control.** These dream clients want to create order from chaos. They achieve this by implementing systems (ruler), providing a duty of care (caregiver), or inventing solutions where the structure determines the outcome (innovator).

When choosing your dream client's archetype, think about who cares for your solution, and make an educated choice that describes how this person might typically behave.

There's no wrong answer. The archetype you choose here will inform your brand story. We'll use this choice to reverse-engineer this type of person into your brand story, so we can spark a reaction in the dream client's monkey brain and inspire it to buy your products and services.

CHAPTER 8

CREATING EMOTIONAL MAPS

'Imagination is everything. It is the preview of life's coming attractions.' - Albert Einstein, genius extraordinaire

By this stage of the journey you should have a clear idea of what your business does and who you do it for. You'll have chosen your Ikigai product or service – the thing that brings both money and joy – and you'll have a good understanding of what your solution does for people who have a common problem.

Using a series of who-cares questions, you'll have narrowed down your target audience to the type of person that cares about your solution. This has produced a mission statement for your business.

For our travel agent who books luxury hotels, the mission statement we created identifies who cares about luxury hotels.

We defined the general target market as ambitious people who don't get enough free time to themselves to enjoy quality experiences. We wrote this mission statement for the travel agent's business:

'I help ambitious people to take proper breaks through booking luxury hotels.'

The mission statement gives us a basis for some intelligent choices about who to design into the business. We know that people have deep psychological needs in the reptilian brain, rational thought in the everyday brain, and impulsive decision-making abilities in the monkey brain.

When the everyday brain creates situations that fail to meet the reptilian brain's deep psychological need for independence, recognition, social belonging, or control, then the monkey brain makes an impulsive purchase to rebel against the everyday brain and keep the reptile happy.

Remember, the monkey and the reptile work together to give the reptile what it needs. If we show the customer how their everyday jackass is sabotaging what they really need, then we can give their monkey brain our nice shiny solution to meet that need, and they will buy your solution every time.

A careful combination of choosing who you want to work with, and empathising with the person who cares about your solution in your mission statement, lets us make an educated decision about what our dream client's reptilian brain most likely needs.

We've also identified what the monkey brain likes and how the dream client achieves their core psychological need. This lets us choose the dream client's archetype, which is a simplified outline of how people with that archetype will typically react to uncomfortable situations.

In Enriched Marketing, we're going to reverse-engineer this type of archetype into the brand story by highlighting how the brand satisfies the client's deepest need, using language that speaks to precisely the right type of person.

It's a very simple model of trigger-reward happiness in consumer decision-making. Rational thought is triggered by highlighting an uncomfortable problem to the dream client. The client's monkey brain makes an impulsive decision to buy your solution that can rectify the problem. The reptilian brain rewards the dream client with feelings of happiness because its core needs are being met, and harmony is restored.

For our travel agent, there are two good ways we could have chosen the dream client's archetype. Ambitious people are frequently driven by independence and the need to free themselves to reach their full potential. Ambitious people also often like recognition and want to leave a mark on the world. For this client, we could have chosen either independence or recognition as the core need.

Our mission statement says that our target audience needs a proper break, and values quality experiences.

If we work with the mindset that our ambitious people are most strongly driven by independence, then we could say that people in this group who value quality experiences likely also want to enjoy life's simple pleasures, and will seek to find inner peace and happiness. This is the innocent archetype.

Had we gone with the other group and said that ambitious people desire recognition, then somebody who works too hard and struggles to take a proper break, and values quality, would be the hero archetype.

The answer you choose is just a starting point that you'll develop your brand around, so don't get too hung up on it at this stage. You're simply making an intelligent choice to decide which type of person you would ideally like to design into the business. Who do you think will best set you up for success?

The trick is to consider your options carefully, but don't overthink it. Your gut feeling is usually the right choice, but if you do later realise you've made the wrong choice then you can always go back a few steps and rework your dream client into something more suitable before you write your sales pages.

Once the archetype is decided, we will use this person's typical psychological triggers to create a herd mentality amongst all people who share a similar psychological make-up. This will cause other people who can relate to the dream client to seek you out, which grows your business by attracting the right clients, and filtering out the wrong clients who waste your time and resources.

When this happens, you reach a place of Enriched Marketing, where the business grows because each and every person who comes into your business ecosystem makes a valuable contribution, and brings both money and joy into your business to achieve the very best results for your clients.

Remember, Enriched Marketing has selling with care at the heart of its philosophy. You must care deeply about who you work with, and you must also care deeply about the people. There's a fine line between leveraging human psychology in marketing, and just manipulating people to do what you want them to do.

The techniques are the same, and they're powerful!

In ethical marketing, the intention behind any psychological sales strategy must be to deliver something that always and only has the client's best interests in mind.

Sell with care.

MAP YOUR 4-POINT STORY

Once we know who the target client is, we can start to unravel the human triggers that drive that particular person's inherent decision-making process. Before we start writing a long sales page, it's best to write a very short story that will become the bones of your entire brand story.

This short story has just four parts, and can be used as your elevator pitch or as inspiration for your organic marketing campaigns. It can be spun into ads, expanded out into website pages, or used as it is in networking chats to sum up who you are in just one paragraph.

It's much easier to write any kind of content for your business when the emotional map is transformed into a short story because you're not reinventing the wheel for everything.

Think of the 4-point story as a roux in a sauce. When you make a sauce, you mix butter and flour together to form a roux, then you add milk and whatever you want into that mixture to make the sauce of your choice.

The roux is the base, and everything else comes from there. It doesn't matter if you make cheese sauce, pepper sauce, mushroom sauce, or jalapeno sauce, it all comes from the same ball of floury butter.

Your emotional map and the 4-point story that comes from it is your roux for all future sales and marketing communications. We write the 4-point story for the target dream client, and that produces the right structure for a long-term communication strategy that draws the right people into your business ecosystem by design.

To make our 4-point story, we need to map the dream client's emotional drivers in relation to your Ikigai service or product. There are four important emotions in the story: hope, fear, dream, and desire.

HOPE

Hope speaks to the instant gratification. What does the monkey get when it buys your service?

Using a quick brainstorming exercise, make a list of the instant gratifications that your solution delivers in the first few minutes or days after the purchase is made.

For our travel agent, we can say that the instant gratifications include:

- A booked holiday
- The promise of a break

- Something to look forward to

- The opportunity to stay in a quality hotel

- The luxury of being looked after for a change

Now, think about your target dream client's archetype and choose the strongest instant gratification from your brainstormed list.

For an innocent dream client who is on a quest to find paradise, the instant gratification in this list will be the promise of a break. This is because innocent archetypes are driven by their sense of independence, so taking a break frees them from working too hard.

If we chose the hero archetype, then the instant gratification will be the opportunity to stay in a quality hotel, because heroes like recognition, and staying in a quality hotel brings high-level social status.

For our travel agent, the innocent dream client will say, I hope for a break. The hero dream client will say, I hope there's a quality hotel.

Dream

The dream emotion refers to the goal the client will fulfil when they buy the instant gratification. Think about the bigger goals that somebody who cares about your solution may have.

In the travel agent example, we know that ambitious people who struggle to find time for a break care about booking luxury hotels. What might their goals look like?

Using the same brainstorming technique, we could say the client's dreams or goals include:

- Time to relax

- Better relationships with others when I'm less stressed

- The opportunity to enjoy life without working so hard

- A refreshed mindset, so that I can push myself with new energy

- Giving myself a treat for all my hard work

If we chose the innocent archetype, then it's likely that their goal is to find an opportunity to enjoy life without working so hard. If we chose the hero archetype, then it's more likely that the client is looking for a refreshed mindset so they can return to work with renewed energy.

Think about the archetype you have chosen in relation to who cares about your service, and choose the strongest relevant goal from your own list.

For our travel agent, the innocent dream client will say, I want to enjoy my life. The hero dream client will say, I want to refresh my energy.

FEAR

The dream client's fear is comprised of two fears which hold them back from saying yes or no to you. This can sometimes cause an internal conflict in the client, so as with all elements of Enriched Marketing, it's important to choose the strongest fears.

The first fear is the fear of saying yes. What can go wrong if they buy this service? For our travel agent, a list of yes fears may look like this:

- What if the travel agent is too expensive?

- What if the travel agent sends me to the wrong place?

- What if I don't enjoy myself?

- What if travelling is too stressful?

- What if the level of luxury is not what I expect it to be?

The second fear is the fear of saying no. What will happen if they don't buy the service? For our travel agent, a list of no fears may look like this:

- If I don't take a break, will I hit burnout?

- If try to do it myself, will I choose the wrong hotel?

- Will it cost me more money if I don't get help with the planning?

- What if I overlook an important detail?

- Will I miss out on something good if I don't ask for advice?

Your target dream client will have a strong, resounding fear for the yes and no responses, which will depend on what their archetype is.

If we're using the innocent archetype for our travel agent, then it's very likely that their fear will be related to not enjoying themselves because an innocent's need is to reach paradise. They likely also fear reaching burnout, because innocents don't like to feel overwhelmed.

The innocent may say, I worry that I won't enjoy myself, but if I don't say yes, I worry that I will reach burnout.

If we're using the hero archetype, then it's more likely that our travel agent's dream client will fear issues with quality and skill.

The hero may say, I worry the travel agent will send me to the wrong place, but what will happen if I do it myself and overlook an important detail?

When you think about your dream client's fears, choose the overarching fears that play into the archetype's typical behaviours in uncomfortable situations. Always pick the strongest fears for the yes and no responses.

DESIRE

The dream client's emotional desire taps into why it really matters to them. When they get the instant gratification from your solution, and achieve their goal, how will that contribute towards their lifelong quest to fulfil their deep psychological need?

The answer to this question lies in the qualities of the archetype itself.

For the innocent archetype, buying the travel agent's service gives them the freedom to enjoy life's simple pleasures without the stress of working too hard. For the hero, buying the travel agent's service lets them refresh themselves with a much-needed break, so they can return home better equipped to leave a quality mark on the world.

Use your chosen archetype to complete the below sentence:

'Using my service lets my dream client (do what their archetype needs), to gain (independence, recognition, social belonging, or control).'

BRING IT TOGETHER TO CREATE A 4-POINT BRAND STORY ROUX

Once you have the ingredients for your story, we need to combine them into a compelling emotional story that will form the base for your future marketing communication sauce. This base foundation places the dream client's psychological decision-making process at the heart of the story, which makes selling to them very easy.

Follow the basic formula for putting together your 4-point brand story, then use it as your elevator pitch whenever somebody asks you what you do.

Here's the formula:

We help (who cares) to (hope/instant gratification), so you can (dream/goal) to (get desire/why it matters) without (fear).

For our travel agent, the 4-point story for a target dream client with the innocent archetype might look like this:

We help ambitious people to book luxury hotels, so you can take a break to enjoy life's little moments without hitting burnout.

For the hero, the 4-point story may look more like this:

We help ambitious people to book quality hotels, so you can refresh your energy without missing out on all the best experiences.

In both of these examples, we're selling the same solution to the same types of people who share the same common problem, but we're creating a whole different feel for the business, which will bring a whole different group of clients into your client base.

Innocent and hero archetypes are very different types of people, and will make for a very different experience when dealing with your clients every day.

People who embrace the innocent archetype are motivated by finding the little pleasures in simple moments. They're pure at heart, with an easy-breezy nature that's light and playful. In stark contrast, people who have the hero archetype are driven to find perfection in the details.

If you take a gentle, easy-breezy approach with people who focus on mastering the details, then your business will struggle to create the right experience for your clients. This will ultimately cause you to feel frustrated by people who make you work too hard for too little reward.

On the other hand, if you take a focused, detail-orientated approach with people who look for soft, gentle experiences, then your business will drive people away because they'll feel that you don't provide the right level and care and comfort in your customer experience.

Tailoring the client's experience to suit their archetype at every stage of the process is crucial to success. Your island of light and joy needs to look like somewhere the dream client would love to be. Your bridge needs to show them what to expect when they get there.

The sign pointing to your bridge on the land of darkness and confusion should give a sense of what it will feel like to step onto your bridge, cross your brand story, and reach a place where all their reptilian dreams can be met with open arms.

The purpose of getting this story right at a foundation level is to create a shared identity amongst the people who can relate perfectly to your style of working, so you can fill your business ecosystem with the people who are best equipped to set you up for success from the outset.

When you get the roux for your brand story right, you can make the perfect sauce. This builds a solid foundation into your business design, and your profits can grow because people become willing to spend their top dollar to receive your best results. The reputation this helps you develop brings more dream clients into your business ecosystem, so the virtuous cycle of money and joy continues.

Reverse-engineering does the opposite of saying yes to everybody. When you say yes to everybody, you fuel a cycle where everybody takes something different from your business, without making a solid contribution to your long-term business objectives.

With a reverse-engineered story, the bad clients don't ask for your help, so you get to fill your business with people who give you both money and joy, and make a positive contribution towards your overall business goals.

Key takeaways

When buying goods and services, people are guided by four emotions, which are their hopes, dreams, fears, and desires.

To create a 4-point brand story that can be built on throughout your marketing campaigns, you should brainstorm each emotion and choose the strongest element from each category.

Hope is the instant gratification that your product or service brings today, and dreams are the goals the client can fulfil when they get the instant gratification.

Fears have two parts. The yes fear describes what the client is afraid will go wrong if they say yes. The no fear describes what the client fears if they don't say yes. Choose the strongest.

The emotional map is informed by the typical behaviours of your chosen archetype.

Archetype thinking can sell the same product or service with the same solution to the same target audience using a very different style. This is what filters bad clients from good clients, and this is how we design the right types of people into your future client base.

Write your 4-point brand story using the formula below, and keep it up your sleeve. This is your elevator pitch!

We help (client type) looking for (hope/instant gratification) to reach your (dream/goal) so you can (get what you desire/why it matters) without (fear).

We will build this out into a website sales page once we've got the marketing information we need to include in the sales journey. We'll do this in the next chapter.

CHAPTER 9

WRITE YOUR BASIC SALES PAGE

'When I write an advertisement, I don't want you to tell me that you find it 'creative.' I want you to find it so interesting that you buy the product.' - David Ogilvy, the father of advertising

A t this stage of the process, we know that your mission statement describes what your Ikigai service is, what it delivers, and who cares about having it. We also know why that outcome matters to the person who cares.

We've used this important information to choose a suitable archetype (for our travel agent, we chose the 'innocent' and the 'hero' as examples), and we've mapped the emotional needs of our dream client.

We're now ready to apply this psychological profile to our sales strategy, and can use the information to write a persuasive sales page for our Ikigai service. This is a basic sales page which follows a formulaic framework, so for now, we're just going to put the structure in place to create something simple.

Later, when we've added depth into your brand personality, we'll expand on this basic structure to personalise the sales page to your business. For now, we're only looking at the structure, which looks like this in a 9-step flow.

1. Headline

2. Introduction

3. Scientific proof

4. Offer details

5. Social proof

6. Add value

7. Reverse risk

8. Call to action

9. Urgency or scarcity

To guarantee that our sales strategy will be successful, we also need to recognise that people will only say yes to a buying decision when all three of the below criteria have been met.

- Buyers must recognise you can help them.
- Buyers must believe you understand them.
- Buyers must see themselves reflected in you.

To achieve this, we'll weave the work we've already done to identify our dream client's deep psychology and to map their emotions into the basic sales page for your business.

When all three of these criteria have been met, then all you need to do is tell people precisely what they should do to get whatever it is you offer, and the right types of clients who resonate with your sales page will come to you.

When buyers need help solving a problem, they should automatically understand that you can help them. If they want to book a hotel, they will naturally recognise that a travel agent who books hotels can help. That one is easy.

Buyers must also believe you understand them. This is where we use the reptilian element of archetype thinking to show the dream client that you really *do* understand what they need. For our heroes, they're booking a hotel, but they really need to feel recognised or important. For our innocents, they're booking a hotel, but they really need to feel independent.

Lastly, buyers must see themselves reflected in you. This is where we use the monkey-brain element of archetype thinking to show the client that you know how they like to fulfil their deep psychological needs. For our heroes, they like mastery, so we'll show them we're masters at booking luxury hotels. For our innocents, they like life's little joys, so we'll show them we know how to facilitate blissful moments at luxury hotels.

Think about what your business does, and how your dream clients like to feel when they interact with you. We'll use this insight to write a winning sales page.

Sales campaigns are formulaic.

They call out the dream client, pull on their emotional heartstrings, and tell people how to act. I'm a big fan of using sales frameworks and copywriting formulas to develop persuasive sales pages, because they work every time with proven results.

I've successfully used these frameworks for more than 100 brands with extraordinary results, and I've developed these techniques through genuine copywriting experience gained in the real world, writing for high-value clients that rake in millions of dollars of worldwide revenues.

Writing a compelling sales campaign is much like baking perfect chocolate chip cookies on a rainy Sunday. If you put the right ingredients into your bowl, mix everything together in just the right way, bake them at precisely the right temperature, and serve them to someone who likes chocolate chip cookies, you'll get a positive result.

If you try to wing it without using the recipe, then you'll probably just get one of those giant flat cookies that takes up the whole tray and ends up uneaten in the bin.

Baking is a precise art. So is selling on paper.

Every sales campaign you write must have these nine elements, which should be blended together using the information you've generated throughout this book, and presented in the correct order to achieve a positive response.

Once you've written your full campaign using the below framework, you can pluck parts of it out to create smaller milestones, shorter ads and easier social media posts. Ultimately, everything you post should start from your sales campaign.

Don't worry if you're not much of a writer. The best writing uses few words, draws from pre-existing knowledge, and follows a predictable format.

But before we start, let's take a quick recap of the travel agent's sales page ingredients. I'll use the innocent and hero archetypes as examples.

We said in the mission statement:

'I help ambitious people to take proper breaks through booking luxury hotels.'

We then made a best-guess choice that the dream client for this travel agent is either going to be an innocent or a hero archetype.

The innocent archetype needs to feel independent in the reptilian brain. They're driven by a sense of safety, and want to enjoy an easy, blissful life where they can appreciate the little moments.

We can spark an innocent archetype into action by showing how the everyday jackass is putting them at risk of burnout (or something unsafe), and present the monkey brain with a shiny version of living a free, easy life.

The hero archetype needs to be recognised for the impact they can make, and the mark they can leave. They're driven by a need to be the best. They master their skills until they reach the pinnacle of success.

We can spark a hero archetype into action by showing how the everyday jackass is failing to reach its full potential (or lacks quality in something). We can present the hero monkey with shiny tools to help the hero achieve their best.

For the innocent, we crafted this emotional map:

We help ambitious people (who cares) to book luxury hotels (hope/instant gratification) so you can take a break (dream/goal) to enjoy life's little moments (desire/why it matters) without hitting burnout (fear).

For the hero, we created this emotional map:

We help ambitious people (who cares) to book quality hotels (hope/instant gratification) so you can refresh your energy (desire/why it matters) without missing out on all the best experiences (fear).

Now, let's write a persuasive sales page for the hero and the innocent using our 9-step sales page structure.

You'll notice that there is sometimes some overlap between the two archetypes, and that's ok. There can be a blend of two or even three archetypes in some of your sales strategies, but the headlines and offer details must sway towards the strongest archetype for maximum effect.

Step 1- Headline

Call out your dream client with a catchy headline. When it comes down to it, the people you want to serve are only looking for somebody who can help them, so your headline's only job is to identify you as someone who can help the dream client.

If we think back to the monkey, the reptile, and the everyday jackass, this is where we show the everyday jackass that the reptile is not getting what it needs.

This is achieved in one of two ways. You can either:

- Establish the underlying problem as a question

Or:

- Make getting the underlying desire newsworthy

Your choice is guided by the customer's level of awareness. If they know the problem exists, go with option one. If they don't yet know they have their problem, go with option two.

For an innocent who knows the problem exists, we can say, 'Feeling stuck in a rut?' for option one, or for the innocent who isn't sure what the problem is, we can say, 'Experience simple, stress-free holidays' for option two.

For the hero who knows what their problem is, we might say, 'Struggling to take a proper break?' for option one. For the hero who doesn't know the problem exists, we can say, 'Reach your full potential with a well-earned break!'

You just want to highlight the essence of what the problem is, or what can be achieved when the problem is solved, for whatever your business does.

It doesn't matter if you sell software or scented candles, the process for getting to the heart of your dream client's deep psychology is the same. If you switch the travel product for a scented bath salt, or deliver a tool that gets people out of a daily rut, the message is the same, because we're speaking to people who need quality and recognition, or to people who need independence to enjoy life's moments of bliss.

What your business does is actually irrelevant. All that matters is what the result delivers, who cares about getting that outcome, and why it matters to the people who care.

STEP 2 - INTRODUCTION

Mirror your dream client's core need to create a sense of belonging. If they seek freedom, make your text feel free. If they need control, make your text feel controlled.

Your introductory paragraph speaks to the lowest level of awareness, and is here to provide a very quick overview of who you help and what you do for them. You want your reader to glance over this paragraph, have their a-ha moment, and keep reading!

- Tell the dream client what you do and who you do it for.

- Highlight the instant gratification your service brings, which is the strongest hope element in your emotional map.

Top Tip! Step 2 is your 4-point story.

For the innocent, we can say, 'We help ambitious people to book quality hotels, so you can take a break to enjoy life's little moments without hitting burnout.'

For the hero, we can say, 'We help ambitious people to book quality hotels, so you can refresh your energy without missing out on all the best experiences.'

STEP 3 - SCIENTIFIC PROOF

Establish your industry-relevant credibility. What have you learned through process, experience, or industry-relevant accreditation that can demonstrate your expertise?

What tangible proof can you show that will make your intangible promise believable? Why can you be trusted to deliver results, and what measurable proof do you have that can back that up?

Here, you want to repackage the three strongest yes fears (what will go wrong if I say yes?) as positive bullet points. For our travel agent, we identified the strongest common yes fears for our archetypes as:

- What if the travel agent sends me to the wrong place?

- What if I don't enjoy myself?

- What if the level of luxury is not what I expect it to be?

We can repackage these fears as three USP-style bullet points by reframing them as positives like this:

- Enjoy our prized locations

- Experience personalised travel

- Discover premium luxury

Top Tip! Start each bullet point with a verb.

STEP 4 – OFFER DETAILS

Give your dream clients a mouth-watering offer they can't refuse. This section speaks to the client's dreams and goals. It should also tap into their underlying desire.

If we think back to the monkey, the reptile, and the everyday jackass, this is where we show the monkey something shiny and tell it how the shiny thing will please the reptile.

Top Tip! Repackage your no fears (what if I don't do it?) as positive benefits.

Write a short paragraph to summarise some of the benefits of your offer in relation to some of your dream client's strongest no fears. For our travel agent, the no fears were:

- If I don't take a break, will I hit burnout?

- If try to do it myself, will I choose the wrong hotel?

- Will it cost me more money if I don't get help with the planning?

- What if I overlook an important detail?

- Will I miss out on something good if I don't ask for advice?

For the innocent, who values feeling safe with a strong sense of finding life's little joys, we can say, 'Book your idyllic escape with someone who really cares, so you can enjoy all the little things with complete peace of mind.'

For the hero, who values quality experiences and the thrill of recognition, we can say, 'Indulge in personalised travel experiences with top-quality luxury, so you can refresh your mind, body, and soul at the perfect hotel.'

STEP 5 – SOCIAL PROOF

What are others saying about you?

People like to know that your previous clients have had a good outcome, so show what others are saying in a collection of testimonials.

If you have many testimonials, try to choose those that highlight how people who resemble your dream client responded to your services. For our travel agent, we may choose testimonials that are similar to this:

'We had the best time, with wonderful experiences!'

'Our hotel was superb!'

'The location was excellent. We loved being so close to everything without losing our sense of exclusivity!'

Top Tip! Like facts, testimonials gain more power when they're specific and measurable, so try to include the person's full name, job title, location, and business name if they agree.

STEP 6 - ADD VALUE

What can you do to sweeten the deal?

Your bonus offer shows why you are worth the spend right now, today.

At this stage of the consumer's thought process, the monkey wants to say yes, but the everyday jackass is putting up some obstacles. The client is looking for something specific in your offer that makes it a no-brainer to say yes.

The best way to solve this is to make your shiny offer even shinier through added value. Go back to the fears and see where you can create extra value for your dream clients to combat some of their strongest fears. Try to choose the fears you haven't yet addressed elsewhere.

For our travel agent, we may like to add value around:

- What if the travel agent is too expensive?

- What if the level of luxury is not what I expect it to be?

- What if I overlook an important detail?

So using these fears, we could add three bonus benefits which say something like the below for an innocent who values an easy life:

- Best rates on the market

- Free room upgrades

- Easy airport transfers

For the hero who values quality and recognition, we may instead say:

- Exclusive offers
- Premium room upgrades
- Luxury airport transfers

This is again just repackaging the fear as a positive benefit for choosing you. Why does the dream client worry about that, and what can you include that will ease their concerns?

Top Tip! Create value offers that complement your main offer. If you're selling bath salts, you may like to add a scented candle or a relaxing music playlist. If you're selling a professional service, you might add a valuable resource that boosts results, or a short course in a closely related subject.

Step 7 – Remove risk

What's the dream client's get-out-of-jail-free card if you fail to deliver?

For most businesses, the easiest way to remove risk is to offer some kind of money-back guarantee if things don't go to plan, but every business is different, so you can be creative with this.

Some ideas that frequently work well for a wide range of industries include:

- Cancel any time

- 30-day money-back guarantee

- Insurance-backed protection

- Regulated by a professional body

- Buy now, pay later

People just need to know there's an exit strategy if a fire breaks out and you disappear with all their money. Our goal here is to create peace of mind.

For our travel agent, our dream client is worried about the cost, so we might say something like:

- Low deposits

- Secure payment gateways

- ATOL and ABTA-protected (these are regulatory bodies in the UK)

Put their hearts at ease by intentionally removing their reasons to say no.

You'll also want to give this section a nice heading, similar to your headline. For the innocent, you might say, 'Soak up life's precious moments at a luxurious hotel.' For the hero, you might say, 'Unwind in the lap of luxury.'

Step 8 - Call to action

It would be a terrible shame to do all this hard work, then lose the client because they don't know what to do next.

Your call to action (CTA) should be short, clear, specific, and obvious. Tell people what they must do to get your product or service. For a travel agent, we may write:

- Enquire here

- Book it

- Call us

For other businesses you may say things like, 'Book a discovery call,' or 'Request a sample or demo.'

The call to action's only job is to specifically tell people what their monkey brain must do to get whatever it is you're offering.

It usually says a variation of, 'Click this shiny button to take the next step in the buying process.'

Step 9 - Urgency or scarcity

How can you add a little bit of genuine time or scarcity pressure to create action?

People are master procrastinators, so if you just say they should do something but don't give a tangible deadline, then it becomes too easy to get distracted and forget about it.

Urgency and scarcity refer to deadlines and limitations. You either need to tell people when to act by, or let them know that there is limited availability.

For our travel agent, we may say something like:

- Enquire today

- Book now

- Offer valid until Friday

Other businesses may say things like, 'Available to the first 100 applicants,' or 'Limited seats, act fast.'

Top Tip! Never use fake urgency to scare people into action! It must be genuine.

You do need to have some urgency in your sales process, but this must be in the client's best interest, not yours. This time sensitivity is there to stop people from procrastinating. It's there to make sure they say yes and don't lose out on the priceless desires your service will bring when they *finally* achieve their goals. It's not there to sell with fear.

The urgency must be real, and it must be in the client's best interest to act fast. If it's not, you'll come off as the sleazy scam and all the effort you've put into crafting the perfect sales campaign will fall flat on its face.

You can tell people to hurry while stocks last if you have limited stock. You can say your cart closes on Friday, but then you must close it on Friday. If the cheaper price is only valid today, then tomorrow it must be more expensive.

There's nothing worse than buying a product on a limited–time offer, and then seeing the same ad for a 'last chance to buy the same thing at a lower price' every week for the rest of time.

Never use fake urgency! Fake urgency is the modern-day version of the boy who cried wolf.

These brands and email marketing gurus who send you urgent reminders for the last chance to get the thing that's always going to be there just cry wolf. Unfortunately, this approach is a huge influencer in modern marketing, and is largely the reason why consumers don't trust the internet.

In my opinion, brands that cry urgency wolf are often the first to go belly up when people lose trust in their credibility. Customers are smart, so honesty is always best.

If you don't have a set closing date, and if your product is always the same price, then the best way to add some urgency is to tell people to act now or call today.

BRING IT ALL TOGETHER

We've looked at how to write a basic sales page based on knowing what the business does, what the dream client's archetype is, and how their emotions relate to whatever it is you're selling.

Earlier, I told you that there would be some crossover between some archetypes in the standard sections of your sales page, but that you should harness your dream client in the headings and offers.

We used the travel agent as the example, and made two versions for an innocent and a hero archetype. You should now have a short, well-structured sales page that can be deepened later when you work your personality into the story.

Let's take a look at the two basic sales pages we've created for the innocent and hero archetypes. Pay attention to how they say the same thing, but speak to two fundamentally different types of people.

<u>Version 1, for the innocent archetype:</u>

Experience Simple, Stress-Free Holidays

We help ambitious people to book quality hotels, so you can take a break to enjoy life's little moments without hitting burnout.

- Enjoy our prized locations
- Experience personalised travel
- Discover premium luxury

Book your idyllic escape with someone who really cares, so you can enjoy all the little things with complete peace of mind.

'We had the best time, with wonderful experiences!' - Jane Doe at Awesome Coach Limited, London

- Best rates on the market
- Free room upgrades
- Easy airport transfers

Soak up life's precious moments at a luxurious hotel.

Low deposits with secure payment gateways. ATOL and ABTA-protected.

Book now!

Version 2, for the hero archetype:

Struggling To Take A Proper Break?

We help ambitious people to book quality hotels, so you can refresh your energy without missing out on all the best experiences.

- Enjoy our prized locations
- Experience personalised travel
- Discover premium luxury

Indulge in personalised travel experiences with top-quality luxury, so you can refresh your mind, body, and soul at the perfect hotel.

'The location was excellent. We loved being so close to everything without losing our sense of exclusivity!' - Joe Soap, Banker, Edinburgh

Unwind in the lap of luxury!

Low deposits with secure payment gateways. ATOL and ABTA-protected.

Enquire today!

This outline forms the bones of your sales page, and can also be used to create other sales pitches, such as video sales letters and social media ads.

You can add much more to each section to make it a longer sales story, for example, in a pitch deck or quote proposal. You can also reduce it right down to just the headings to make it short and snappy.

When selling through written words, the key to success is to keep the flow of information in the same order presented here, because this follows our natural decision-making process, and is therefore the most persuasive way to deliver your sales pitch to your potential clients.

In the next section, we'll develop your brand's values and personality, then we'll go back into this basic sales page to give it the right character for your brand.

SECTION 3

DEFINING YOUR BRAND'S PERSONALITY

CHAPTER 10

THE GOLDEN MOMENT OF ENRICHED MARKETING

'One of the deep secrets of life is that all that is really worth the doing is what we do for others.' - Lewis Carroll

Until now, everything we've done in this book has been about finding out who your dream client is, how your business serves them, and why it matters to them.

We'll now use this knowledge to inform what your brand needs to become to attract those types of people. In this section, we'll work through your business values to create an island of light and joy that looks appealing to the right types of clients.

I'd like to take a moment to highlight the golden moment here: the thing that makes this method so successful.

In Enriched Marketing, we first figure out who the dream

client is, how we can best serve them, and why it matters to them. *Then* we create a business and brand story where that person's needs are met at every level of our customer experience.

It's not about us; it's about what we do for *them*.

This is very different to conventional business building and regular marketing, and is the driving force behind why Enriched Marketing creates such powerful brands.

Conventional businesses and those who use normal marketing methods usually start by deciding what the business wants to be. These businesses will oftentimes first identify their USPs and competitive advantages, and will then create a narrative that differentiates the business from others like it.

When the brand and business structure is established on the business owner's terms, these conventional brands usually then go out and try to market the business to whoever will buy into it. They make tacky sales campaigns that can feel sales-y, or they experience mixed results that can't be easily predicted. These brands inevitably fold into failure or go through a major, oftentimes expensive, rebrand.

In Enriched Marketing, we use our understanding of the dream client to create a world that is so richly rewarding for the people we want to fill it with, that they come to us autonomously and struggle to walk away from us.

The right clients are naturally drawn towards enriched brands because they know from the outset that their deepest needs will be met by a business that truly understands them.

This is crucial to wrap your head around, because for the next few chapters we'll build your brand story on the dream client's terms, and not your own, which may at times feel uncomfortable or counterintuitive. But it is fundamentally the golden moment behind why this method of Enriched Marketing is so powerful.

It works the same way for all businesses, in every industry, regardless of what you sell or who you sell it to, because it puts the dream client at the heart of your brand story and designs a business that was built to serve them.

If you want to attract people who value structure and order, then you need to create an island of light and joy that looks like a structured place from miles away. If you want to attract people who value rebellion, then you need to look like an outlaw from as far as the eye can see.

This is where conventional marketing often fails. People build brands that look like chaos because they want their brand to 'be edgy,' then they wonder why they fail to win innovative clients who value structure and seek control.

If your dream client feels even for a moment that your business is misaligned with who they are in their deep psychology, you will inadvertently cause them to feel uncomfortable before they give you the chance to show them what you can do to serve them.

When your dream client sees you from afar and recognises that your brand aligns comfortably with their core values, they will assume you're the right person to help them, and they'll be willing to pay more just for the opportunity to choose you.

Apple users buy Apple products. They don't throw a passing glance at the competition because when all the other tech companies out there were focusing on how to differentiate themselves from the competition, Apple was focusing on how to resonate with the people they wanted to serve.

Today, Apple users are the picture of brand loyalty. At the time of writing this book, the Apple Inc. brand is worth 2.7 trillion dollars.

The principles in this book are the very same principles used by Apple.

Enriched Marketing puts the client first, and always acts to serve the client's needs above all else. If you get this right, you can design a brand that's filled with all the best people who naturally set you up for success. They bring their friends, they sing your praises, they deepen your pockets, and most of all, they stay loyal to your brand for a lifetime.

CHAPTER 11

THE WORLD'S MOST
POWERFUL WORD

'There are only two ways to influence human behavior: you can manipulate it or you can inspire it.' - Simon Sinek, author of *Start With Why*

In 1978, Ellen Langer of Harvard University conducted a simple Xerox experiment to understand the complexities of social behaviours around doing favours for others.* The experiment hypothesised that people respond to requests differently depending on the size of the favour asked for, and the reason for asking.

Three groups of people were instructed to cut the line at a

---

* Langer, E., Blank, A.E. and Chanowitz, B. (1978) 'The mindlessness of ostensibly thoughtful action: The role of 'placebic' information in interpersonal interaction', *Journal of Personality and Social Psychology*, 36(6), pp.635–642. doi:10.1037/0022-3514.36.6.635.

Xerox machine and ask to make 20 photocopies (a small favour), using one of three predetermined excuses:

- Group 1 made a straight-up request with no reason given: 'Excuse me, I have 20 pages. May I use the Xerox machine?'

- Group 2 provided a weak reason with little value: 'Excuse me, I have 20 pages. May I use the Xerox machine, because I have to make copies?'

- Group 3 gave real information with a genuine reason: 'Excuse me, I have 20 pages. May I use the Xerox machine, because I'm in a rush?'

The results were astounding! When asked for small favours, 60% of respondents said yes with no reason given; however, 93% of respondents said yes when given a low-value reason, and 94% said yes when given a genuine reason.

Nearly all respondents who were given any reason why they should say yes responded significantly more positively than those who were not given a reason at all, but the reason itself caused little difference in their willingness to say yes.

Based on Ellen Langer's research, Harvard determined that the mechanism for inspiring a yes response was the *existence* of a reason, not the reason itself. This study has caused the word 'because' to become widely respected as one of the most powerful words in persuasive psychology.* Simply placing the word 'because'

---

* This is hotly debated, but in my professional opinion the word 'because' nearly always changes the outcome of sales campaigns. People buy more when you give them a reason to spend their money.

into a non-descript request can inspire the yes response.

So this is one reason why you want to include your reason why in your sales story. Another reason is because, if you don't, your customers will fill it in for you. In Langer's research, we see that giving a vague reason got a similar response to a valid reason. This is likely because people fleshed out the vague reason in their own minds to fill in the missing details themselves.

We're hardwired to look for patterns, and the human mind is exceptionally good at making up the details when the information is vague or missing.

A good example of this is when we don't notice the details in something obvious. If you look at a wall with ten picture frames on it, it's easy for the mind to read the scene as ten pictures in ten frames and assume that all ten frames are full. But if you look closer, you may well find that two or even three of those frames are completely empty.

So powerful is the human brain's ability to flesh out the details that in sales, all we need do is hint at something and the consumer will fill in the trail of thought with their own embellishments. Your audience can assume something is there when it's not, like pictures in frames.

In brand storytelling, if your reason why is merely implied, then we give the consumer's mind free rein to fill in the details however they wish. This vagueness dilutes your brand's impact, and ultimately, loses trust.

The human brain's extraordinary ability to fill in the missing details makes the word 'because' so effective in branding.

Had we asked the people waiting at the Xerox machine why the person with the excuse needed to make copies, or why that person was in a rush, it's very likely that each waiting person would have made up a different reason for the excuse given. The same happens with incomplete brand stories. If you ask consumers how they interpret a vague brand, chances are good that each person will view the brand differently.

We don't want people making assumptions on what your brand is about and why you can help them – we want to be ultra-specific about why your solution works, why your client will benefit from it, and why your business exists to serve them.

When you actively and specifically tell your dream clients why something is good for them, they stop looking for gaps in your story and trust your business to do what it says on the box.

This creates long-term customer loyalty for all the right reasons.

WHY DO YOU DO WHAT YOU DO?

There is no formula for determining your reason why your island of light and joy exists. This needs to come from you. It should represent the combination of what you do and what you love doing – your passion, and your purpose.

- What gets you up in the mornings to run your business?

- What inspired you to start this business, and why does finding success for your clients matter to you?

- Which journey did you take to get to where you are today?

Brainstorm some ideas around your backstory, and come up with a clear sentence to tell your dream client why you're in this business.

In my own business, for example, I learned how to create niche brands for specific people because I made all the same mistakes that many of my dream clients make, and I experienced a fast, painful fall as a result of getting it wrong.

In 2017, my business goal was to leverage my complex skill set to help everybody with everything. I lazily resurrected my old business name that was once used for a successful photography school I had started back in 2005, Touch Light Studios, and turned it into a 'rounded marketing service for small businesses'. I spent months building out products and packages that I planned to deliver myself because for some reason, I thought I was a unicorn.

Those services included, amongst other things, copywriting, graphic design, ad management, website design, social media, photography, mystery shopping, and non-descript customer experience management.

Six months later, I shut shop and gave up on myself, because despite having over two decades of experience in sales and marketing, I had managed to create *precisely* the type of business that would never work.

I had set myself up to fail, and the failure was spectacular!

Touch Light Studios had been enormously successful as a private photography school in the early 2000s, but didn't manage to invoice a single client as a jack of all trades marketing knick-knack with no clear direction.

An 'always-say-yes' mentality was the reason it failed. I planned to say yes to everybody, so naturally, nobody felt special enough to want me.

When I finally worked out that my purpose is to help people see their own value, I started a copywriting business, and refined my Ikigai service into brand voice development through reverse-engineered brand stories.

I read everything I could find on consumer psychology, and put all the pieces together in a way that helps people to see their own value without falling down the shiny marketing rabbit holes.

I do this because seeing the way people's eyes twinkle when their business falls into place makes my heart feel warm. It plays into my own archetype, the magician, and lets me leave my mark on the world through empowering others to achieve their burning desires.

Your reason why is a significant force in the dream client's yes response. People work with me because it enables them to see all the possibilities in their untapped potential.

To find your reason why, you need to think about the 'because' trigger for both sides of the story.

What's your story? Why are you here, doing what you do, for the people you do it for?

What's your client experience? Why do they love working with you?

A QUICK EXERCISE

Using the same method we used to find out who cares about your service and why it matters, interrogate your mission statement using, 'because …'

For our travel agent, this process may look a bit like this:

I help ambitious people to take proper breaks through booking luxury hotels because …

- I know what it's like to feel burned out. Because …

- I work too hard. Because …

- I'm driven by perfection. Because …

- I like to feel in control of my life. Because …

- It gives me a sense of security. Because …

- I need to feel safe. Because …

- Feeling safe makes it easy to enjoy life's little moments.

We can now bring that together to write a personal mission statement for your business.

I help ambitious people to take proper breaks through booking luxury hotels because I know the value of feeling secure, and I want people to enjoy life's precious moments with complete peace of mind, knowing they're always in safe hands.

Keep this paragraph handy because we'll use it on your about page at the end of this section.

Key takeaway

Your reason why should infiltrate into everything you do. Pin it to your wall, sear it to your heart, and make sure that you *always* know why you are here, doing what you do, serving your dream client with your best Ikigai services.

CHAPTER 12

DEVELOP YOUR BRAND'S CHARACTER

'Everything can be taken from a man but one thing: the last of the human freedoms - to choose one's attitude in any given set of circumstances, to choose one's own way.' - Hector Garcia, author of *Ikigai*

Previously, we've spoken about the difference between archetypes and personalities as the difference between typical behaviours and unique personal characteristics. Brand character is the sum of your brand's archetype, personality, values and style.

Your brand archetype describes your dream client's core need, and how they typically behave to get that need. For example, dream clients who are motivated to leave a mark on the world will typically seek mastery, empowerment, or rebellion to achieve that. This would make their archetype a hero, a magician, or an outlaw.

Your brand personality tells us how you approach things. Your brand values show us what's important to you, and your style shows us what you're like to interact with.

Together, these elements form your unique brand character.

By this stage of the process, you should have a good idea of your dream client's archetype, but it's worth also deciding what your own archetype is, using the same criteria as you used for your dream client.

Just like your clients, you may feel that you're perhaps more than one archetype. That's normal, so just choose the strongest fit. Remember, the archetype is the typical behaviour that you resort to when placed under extreme pressure. The answer should be instinctive, so don't overthink it!

It's important that your brand's archetype and your own archetype have some natural alignment, so that you're not trying to run a business that goes against your natural grain.

When we considered our fictitious travel agent's reason why, we came up with this mission statement:

'I help ambitious people to take proper breaks through booking luxury hotels because I know the value of feeling secure, and I want people to enjoy life's precious moments with complete peace of mind, knowing they're always in safe hands.'

This mission statement focuses on finding security, enjoying life, and feeling safe. That's closely aligned with the innocent archetype, so suggests that the travel agent's own archetype is also innocent. This business would do well to position itself as an innocent brand.

The dream client and the business owner don't always need to be the same archetype, as long as the difference makes sense in the brand–client relationship, and together, the two archetypes for a team that's strong and united.

For example, an innocent brand that values creating blissful moments can very easily be run by somebody with a lover archetype, who looks for pleasure. A ruler brand that delivers a sense of control to its customers can just as easily be managed by somebody with a hero archetype, who looks to master skills and quality.

This natural alignment between the dream client's archetype and your own archetype can make the business stronger, as long as it is a natural alignment and doesn't cause you to go against your grain.

In a different scenario, a ruler who values control may have dream clients that are outlaws. This will be challenging, because the business owner will struggle to understand the rebellious customers, and the customers won't easily feel connected to the rulebound brand.

You don't have to choose dream clients with the same archetype as you, as long as you choose dream clients who will complement your own deep psychological needs.

Much of choosing your archetype and the brand you want to be will come down to following your instinct and choosing the types of people you enjoy working with. But if you think about it intentionally, and if you really dig around in the choices you make, you'll likely find that it's not guesswork at all.

Most business owners share the same archetype as their dream client.

In our fictitious travel agent's example, we said the business owner helps ambitious people to take proper breaks through booking luxury hotels, because they know the value of feeling secure and they want people to enjoy life's precious moments with complete peace of mind, knowing they're always in safe hands.

This travel agent's dream clients will recognise that somebody who understands safety can help them to feel secure, and will self-identify with the shared desire to enjoy life's little moments.

The travel agent is now known to be an innocent archetype, and the dream client also has an innocent archetype.

If we were to choose the hero archetype for the travel agent's dream client (which is also a strong contender), then the dream client will recognise that somebody who is attentive to detail can help them feel safe, even though the business likes to deliver simple moments of joy, and the dream client fundamentally looks for high-quality experiences.

It's close enough, and it works, but for this travel agent an innocent brand story is the stronger choice, and will ultimately attract clients with the innocent archetype, so the correct choice for this business is to build an innocent brand story.

The educated guesswork at the start of the process has been refined by aligning the brand with the business owner, and we now know that we should create the right sense of character for an innocent brand.

There are three aspects of character in every brand story: your personality, your style, and your values.

ASPECT 1 – WHAT'S YOUR BRAND PERSONALITY?

Your personality describes what your overall energy and style is like.

Much of Carl Jung's work is dedicated to understanding how we develop our personalities in relation to the ego, the shadow, the persona, and the self. In other words, who we are, what we hide, how we represent ourselves to others, and what our inner nature is like.

Inspired by Carl Jung, top brand storytellers have since categorised the archetypes into three subcategories, where some are ruled by the head, some by the heart, and some by the soul.

Harley Davidson, an outlaw brand, is instantly recognisable as a soul brand. Dove, an innocent brand, is easily interpreted as a heart brand.

Just like Carl Jung defined and categorised all the world's people into twelve general archetypes with a shared collective unconscious, our brand personalities can also loosely be categorised into just five overarching groups:

- Sophisticated

- Rugged

- Sincere

- Competent

- Excited

Using the five overarching personalities is a good guideline for finding your basic brand personality, and this is easy enough to do with a bit of common sense and logic.

Think about your brand's archetype. Which fundamental brand personality does your archetype lend itself to from the list below?

- The sage, hero, everyman, and ruler are ruled by the head. These archetypes value learning, mastering skills, fitting in, and staying in control. These archetypes are represented by their competency, so lend themselves to a competent personality.

- The magician and the jester are ruled by the heart. These two archetypes want to empower the world around them, and connect with others through living in the moment. They can be seen as excited.

- Innocent and caregiver archetypes are also ruled by the heart, but these archetypes are driven by life's little moments, and looking after others. They are represented by their sincerity.

- The explorer and the outlaw archetypes are ruled by the soul, and these two archetypes are represented by the rugged personality. They're all about getting off the beaten track and challenging the status quo.

- Lovers and innovators are also ruled by the soul. Lovers look for life's pleasures, and innovators look for sleek ways to improve everything they touch, so these two archetypes are represented by sophistication.

For our travel agent with an innocent brand, we'll create a sincere brand personality. In my business, which is a magician brand, I've created an excited brand personality.

We'll now take this foundation and add some layers to the brand's personality to make your business feel unique.

ASPECT 2 – WHAT'S YOUR STYLE?

If you were to take your business out to lunch, where would you go and what would the dress code be?

Think about your business as a person and spend a day with yourself.

Would you go for a picnic in the park and run around in your bare feet without a care in the world, or would you book a smart, upmarket restaurant with fine wines and starched white tablecloths?

Perhaps a trendy cocktail bar with an unrivalled view will suit, or maybe you'll just keep it comfy with your casual jeans in a friendly pub.

What kind of person would your business be? Write down five to ten words that describe them to a stranger.

Let's assume that our travel agent would take their business to lunch at an understated restaurant with a laid-back feel. We might describe someone who would choose to lunch like this as relaxed, approachable, friendly, warm, and open.

If our travel agent instead took their business to lunch in the private cellar of a renowned wine estate, we might describe them as refined, cultured, sophisticated, discerning, or stylish.

There's no right answer here. This is a space for you to really think about how you want to come across to others as a human brand with a human personality.

What's your overall business style?

What can people expect when they come into your ecosystem, walk up to your point of sale, and pay a premium price just for the opportunity to choose you?

For the next minute or two, find a comfortable spot and think about what's most important to you as a person within the context of your business.

Aspect 3 – What do you value?

Our values relate to the beliefs, philosophies, and life experiences that shape the way we hold ourselves accountable.

Take a few minutes to brainstorm the qualities you value within yourself and others. Some examples could include things like courage, curiosity, imagination, or generosity. Write down everything that's important to you and your business.

Everybody has many different values, and some of these values will resonate well with your chosen archetype, while others may not.

For example, you might value courage and conformity. If you have an outlaw brand that's built on rebellion, then courage will sing loudly to your dream client, while conformity will be a hard sell.

Think about your dream client's archetype and choose five values from your list that align best with it. For our travel agent who targets an innocent archetype, we might write:

Simplicity. Purity of heart. Kindness. Compassion. Generosity.

The brand values you choose should answer the question, 'How do I want others to see me?'

In my magician business, my brand values include courage, curiosity, generosity, wonder, and warmth.

BRING IT TOGETHER TO DEFINE YOUR BRAND'S UNIQUE CHARACTER

By working through the four exercises above, we can now define our unique brand personality to suit our reverse-engineered brand story, based on the dream client's archetype.

For our travel agent example, which is an innocent archetype, the overarching brand personality is sincerity. The brand style is understated.

When customers interact with the brand, the energy should feel relaxed, approachable, friendly, warm, and open. The brand values are simplicity, purity of heart, kindness, compassion, and generosity.

From now on, everything the business does should be defined by this brand personality profile. We'll use the information gathered here to write your about page.

CHAPTER 13

YOUR UNIQUE MECHANISM

'A mechanism is a special way of getting something done within a particular system.' - Collins Dictionary

A common mistake people make in marketing is to build their marketing strategy around unique selling points (USPs). This happens because most of the marketing bumf we learn in 'How to Start a Business 101' says that your USPs are what differentiate you from your competition.

They do differentiate you, but the term 'differentiation' is widely and incorrectly interpreted as the thing that makes you better, stronger, or faster than everyone else, when really what differentiates you is the thing that makes you *fundamentally different* from everything else available.

USPs make your description of your business sound like it

should start with 'more' and end in 'er'. 'We're more likely to get results because we're better.'

Your unique mechanism is the unique approach you use in your own process that makes you different to other solutions that achieve the same result. It's the culmination of your learnings, your experience, your research, and your intellectual input. When you focus on your unique mechanism, none of the descriptive words ending in 'er' matter because there's nobody else like you to compare you to.

The weight-loss industry is the poster child for demonstrating the difference between USPs, which are largely irrelevant in marketing, and unique mechanisms, which can change everything in marketing.

It's widely accepted by the World Health Organization and most global health boards that a good way to lose weight is to eat healthier food.

The mechanism for weight loss is to eat better, but there are thousands of businesses that offer better food as a way to lose weight. These are competing businesses. If you look at the marketing landscape, it might look a little like this:

- **Business 1:** Our healthy recipes are the tastiest on the market.

- **Business 2:** Our healthy recipes can be made in less than 30 minutes.

- **Business 3:** Our healthy recipes let you eat whatever you like, as long as you stay within your daily points range.

The customer wants to lose weight, so they look for ways to eat healthier food. All of these businesses get people to lose weight by encouraging them to eat healthier food. Their mechanism for success – eat healthy food – is fundamentally the same, and they use their USPs – their 'er' descriptors – to stand out in a crowded market.

The customer's journey through their weight-loss experience might look a bit like this:

First, they try the 'tastiest' stuff but don't really like it, so it doesn't work. Next, they go with the faster 30-minute meal kits, but those get boring, so that doesn't work either. Then, they try the most flexible 'eat whatever you want' option, but that's hard to keep track of so it fails too.

Eventually, they make peace with being overweight and tell themselves that losing weight is perhaps not worth the effort after all, and they decide that dieting just doesn't work. This customer is difficult to sell to because they assume you will fail if your product looks like yet another USP-inspired way to give them healthier food.

These customers feed a multi-billion-dollar diet industry because they keep failing at the common mechanism used, which is to eat healthier food. That's good for the industry as a whole because they keep buying diet products, but it's bad for individual businesses because customers who fail at your service stop using your products.

In 2008, Noom came onto the market with a different mechanism for eating healthy food. Instead of telling people what to eat, they use cognitive behavioural therapy (CBT) to change the way people think about food. This uses psychology to encourage healthier choices, so the result is that people eat better and lose weight.

The end result is exactly the same – people eat healthier food and therefore lose weight – but the unique mechanism used is fundamentally different.

Using a different mechanism means that Noom doesn't need to highlight why their recipes are more appealing than all the other healthy diets out there. They do things in a different way to overcome the key consumer question, which is, *'Why will it work this time when everything I've tried before to solve this exact same problem has failed me in the past?'*

At the time of writing this book, Noom is valued at 3.7 billion dollars, which is around double that of the best-performing 'er' company that focuses on *what* you can eat to lose weight.

When you focus on your 'er's, your USPs, it doesn't matter how much bigger, better, faster, shinier, friendlier, or trendier you are. If somebody comes along with a different way of achieving your results, and it works, then they will knock you out of the park every time.

If you want to win the marketing game, you need a unique mechanism for achieving results that's fundamentally different to the things your dream clients have tried before.

Your unique mechanism is what lets you rise above their previous failed attempts to solve their underlying problem. It's a promise of hope that this time they will get what they need, because your process for delivering results is different from the other unsuccessful things they have tried before.

To get to your unique mechanism, we need to assess what went wrong for your dream clients. Think about their previous failures within a framework of common obstacles.

- **Time:** Did it take too long to see results? Why?

- **Effort:** Was it too difficult to implement? Why?

- **Cost:** Was it more expensive than they could comfortably afford? Why?

- **Technology:** Did they lack the tools needed to do the work involved? Why?

- **Trust:** Did they lose faith in the product or service before seeing results? Why?

Choose the strongest reason from the list above, and interrogate it until you understand the reason for failure. In the case of the weight-loss industry, conventional diet plans commonly fail because eating healthy food doesn't solve the emotional problem that makes people eat their feelings.

Now, think about why you are different. In the case of Noom, they differentiated themselves by showing that their mechanism addresses the underlying feelings that cause people to have a bad relationship with food.

The unique mechanism is to use CBT to deal with the underlying emotions, which removes the bad relationship and makes healthy eating easier.

You can use the same 'so why?' process we have used previously for your strongest reason for failure. Use the dream client's fears for inspiration.

For our travel agent, the strongest fears were related to missing important details, paying too much, and choosing the wrong hotel. This is likely a technology-related issue where they lack the tools to make a knowledgeable choice, so let's interrogate that. You may also like to repeat the exercise for all of your dream client's fears until you know you have the strongest reason for past failures.

- Why did they fail?
- Because they lack the technology to make the right choices. Why?
- Because they try to book online but they don't know what to look for. Why?
- Because the travel industry is complex, and no booking engine gives all of the information. Why?
- Because online booking sites cater for many different types of people. Why is that a problem?
- Because people have to sift through too much information which gets tedious. Why does it get tedious?
- Because it's overwhelming. Why is it overwhelming?
- Because you don't know what you don't know.

From this interrogation, we can see that the reason why this travel agent's dream clients have likely failed at finding the right hotel before is because people don't know what they don't know, so they don't know what they're looking for when they try to choose a quality hotel.

So, how can we solve that?

- We can have an open conversation to ask the client what's important to them, then use our own knowledge and experience to fill in the gaps in their knowledge.

- We can use sophisticated technology to map out the possibilities within the scope of options that we know are already suitable for them, so they can consolidate the information from a smaller pool of options to make a clear choice.

You may have a much longer list. Choose the strongest reason and interrogate it again with the question, 'Why is that …?' until you have the crux of why your approach to solving your dream client's problem is fundamentally different to your competitors' approach.

For our travel agent, let's use option 1 as the example.

- We can have an open conversation to ask the client what's important to them, then use our own knowledge and experience to fill in the gaps in their knowledge. Why is that different?

- Because I've travelled myself. Why is that different to other agents?

- Because nobody else has experienced travel in the same way that I have. Why is that helpful?

- Because I know what different guest experiences feel like and how that affects people's travel. Why is that helpful?

- Because I can predict what will be suitable for them based on the experiences they value. Why is that valuable to the client?

- Because I can unravel what's really important to them and give them what they really need. Why is that important?

- Because people travel to feel something, but they don't always know what that is when they're planning it. Why does that matter?

- Because travel is emotional, so the best way to experience it is to understand why you want to travel, not where you want to go.

For our travel agent, we can now say that our unique mechanism is to understand why people want to travel, so we can create the right experience from the outset.

In my business, my unique mechanism is to combine archetype-driven brand stories with triune brain theory to inspire the monkey, the reptile and the everyday jackass sales model.

Most marketing companies define your USPs, up your ad spend, change your social media strategy, or redesign your look and feel with a new website. These are just different types of tactics that use 'get more leads' as a mechanism for 'make more money'.

With Enriched Marketing, the unique mechanism doesn't rely on *how many* leads you can get to achieve the result of making more money. Instead, your unique mechanism changes the *types* of leads you bring into your business, so you can increase your average order value to grow your profits without the stress of finding more leads.

Your unique mechanism becomes the 'Why choose us?' section on your about page.

Top Tip! The final answer to this section is nearly always to do with emotions. Everything in life and business ultimately comes down to how we feel, and we can change the way people feel just by changing their experiences.

Keep going until you get to the heart of what really matters, and you'll have a unique mechanism that skyrockets your business into whichever future you want for it.

CHAPTER 14

WRITE YOUR ABOUT PAGE

'Dedicate yourself to a core set of values.
Without them, you will never be able to find
personal fulfillment, and you will never be able to lead
effectively.' – Kenneth Chenault, former CEO of American Express

Just like our basic sales page, the about page on your website is largely formulaic, but it plays a different role, and it should always be a stand-alone page rather than just a part of your longer sales page.

The about page is there to show your dream client who you really are, what you value, and how well you align with their own psychological profile.

Enriched Marketing makes writing an about page very easy, because instead of waffling on about your life story or scratching your head trying to work out what to say about yourself, you need only make yourself look like the brand that your dream client wants you to be.

Reverse-engineering the dream client into your brand story means that we already know who we need to be as a business to attract the right types of people into the business ecosystem.

To look at this a different way, if you want chocolate clients, then you need to make your about page feel chocolatey. If you make it vanilla, you can expect to get vanilla clients. Everything we've done up to here has refined and enhanced your preferred flavour, so all we need to do is put the parts of the reverse-engineered brand story together in the right six-part sequence to create a winning brand.

It looks like this:

1. Headline

2. Purpose

3. Backstory

4. Unique mechanism

5. Credibility

8. Call to action

There's no exact science to writing any content for your business, so play around with the information you've gathered throughout this section until it sounds just right.

As a quick recap, for our travel agent we have said the overarching personality is sincerity. The brand values are simplicity, purity of heart, kindness, compassion, and generosity. When customers interact with the brand, the energy should feel relaxed, approachable, friendly, warm, and open.

The agent's reason why is that they know the value of feeling secure and want people to enjoy life's precious moments with complete peace of mind, knowing they're always in safe hands.

The unique mechanism is to understand why people want to travel, so we can create the right experience from the outset.

We can now use this information to write an about page that is perfect for your dream client.

Step 1 - Headline

Give your readers a sense of belonging with an inspiring headline that taps into their archetype. For our travel agent, the archetype is innocent, so we'll choose something that speaks to somebody who enjoys life's simple pleasures.

We also want to use language that reflects the overarching personality, which is sincerity. For our travel agent, we might write:

'Stay Pure At Heart With Natalie's Travel Agency'.*

Top Tip! Use one of your brand values in your headline.

---

* Any resemblance to any real travel agency is purely coincidental! The example travel agency created for this book is purely fictitious.

Step 2 – Purpose

Your purpose is your reason why you get up in the mornings, so here we just want to write a short introduction to your reason why. For our travel agent, we can say:

'My purpose is to encourage ambitious people to take proper breaks, because I know the value of feeling secure in life and business. I want people to enjoy all of life's precious moments with complete peace of mind.'

Top Tip! Write directly to the reader. You're just going to make minor tweaks to the work you've already done on your why statement, so that it sounds conversational between you and the person you want to say it to.

Step 3 – Backstory

This is where you get to highlight your values and your personality. You want to show the journey you've taken to develop your reason why, and let people know what the experience will be like when they interact with your business.

Go back to the interrogation exercise you did to get to your reason why (your purpose), and turn it into your backstory. For our travel agent, the reason why exercise looked like this:

I help ambitious people to take proper breaks through booking luxury hotels because:

- I know what it's like to feel burned out. Because …

- I work too hard. Because …

- I'm driven by perfection. Because …

- I like to feel in control of my life. Because …

- It gives me a sense of security. Because …

- I need to feel safe. Because …

- Feeling safe makes it easy to enjoy life's little moments.

Using this information, we're going to write a short paragraph to summarise the thought process for getting to your reason why, with a short overview of what you value.

For our travel agent, we might say something like:

'As a small business owner, I know first-hand what it's like to hit mental burnout when we forget to take proper breaks. I'm driven by perfection, so everything I do is designed to stay on top of the little details that can make travel more stressful than it needs to be.

I value simplicity, purity of heart, kindness, compassion, and generosity.

I believe that when everything is taken care of, we can fully relax, and enjoy life's simple pleasures without the overwhelm.'

You'll also want to give this section a nice, archetype-inspired heading. Something like:

'Blissful Experiences, Made Easy'

Top Tip! Write directly to the reader, and keep their archetype's fears and desires in mind to play into the emotional map we created earlier on in the process.

STEP 4 – YOUR UNIQUE MECHANISM

Let your readers see how your unique mechanism adds value to your brand story, and show what the experience is like when they work with you. For our travel agent, we might write:

'Why Choose Me?

My goal is to understand why you want to travel to your preferred destination, so we can create the right experience from the outset. My approach is relaxed and friendly, with a warm atmosphere that encourages openness and approachability.

When you work with me, you can expect to feel welcome, always in safe hands.'

STEP 5 – CREDIBILITY

Establish your authority in your field to build your credibility. This is where you'll outline the learnings and experiences that have shaped your unique mechanism. It's a personal paragraph, but should show recognisable credentials if you have these.

For our travel agent, we might say:

'I've travelled all over the world, and have had the privilege of staying in some of the finest hotels in the best locations. I understand what makes experiences feel special, and I have all the right tools to deliver exceptional travel, wherever it is that you would like to go to.

All travel is ATOL and ABTA-protected, with secure financial backing, and low deposits.'

Top Tip! Pair why you are credible as a person with why the industry respects you, in whichever way is most relevant to your industry.

STEP 6: CALL TO ACTION

Keep this simple and let your dream clients know what to do next with a clear instruction. These are some good ideas:

- Book today

- Enquire now

- Message us here

Just like the sales page, you want to make your call to action verb-heavy, with an actionable timeframe if possible.

Bring it together

For our travel agent example, we'll now have an about page that looks like this:

Stay Pure At Heart With Natalie's Travel Agency

My purpose is to encourage ambitious people to take proper breaks, because I know the value of feeling secure in life and business. I want people to enjoy all of life's precious moments with complete peace of mind.

Blissful Experiences, Made Easy

As a small business owner, I know first-hand what it's like to hit mental burnout when we forget to take proper breaks. I'm driven by perfection, so everything I do is designed to stay on top of the little details that can make travel more stressful than it needs to be.

I value simplicity, purity of heart, kindness, compassion, and generosity. I believe that when everything is taken care of, we can fully relax, and enjoy life's simple pleasures without the overwhelm.

Why Choose Me?

My goal is to understand why you want to travel to your preferred destination, so we can create the right experience from the outset. Our approach is relaxed and friendly, with a warm atmosphere that encourages openness and approachability.

When you work with me, you can expect to feel welcome, always in safe hands.

I've travelled all over the world, and have had the privilege of staying in some of the finest hotels in the best locations. I understand what makes experiences feel special, and I have all the right tools to deliver exceptional travel, wherever it is that you would like to go to.

All travel is ATOL and ABTA-protected, with secure financial backing, and low deposits.

Enquire Today!

A QUICK NOTE ON USING PERSONAL PRONOUNS

Personal pronouns such as 'I' and 'we' can be used flexibly, which has over time caused polarised opinions in the business world. Should you try to sound bigger than you really are by referring to yourself as 'we', or should you keep to a humble 'I' at the risk of looking too small?

This is a personal choice, but in my experience, I think it's best to be guided by individual situations to do what feels right for your business.

'I' is strong. It demonstrates independent thought and shows your authenticity. If you're a solopreneur speaking about what you believe and value, then I think 'I' is best.

However, in most other situations, 'us' and 'we' are generally best because these create inclusion and also feel more credible. If you have at least one other person who genuinely does work in your business, then you can say, 'Why Choose Us?' and 'We believe …'

'We' and 'us' can at times be used alongside 'I', because these personal pronouns can sometimes include the solopreneur and the client as a team of two, which is a great way of putting the client in your corner. 'We're on a mission to help you achieve …' can be quite effective for a solopreneur who goes on a mission to achieve something with the client, as long as it makes sense in context.

Ultimately, this is a choice you need to make for your own business. My best advice is to lean towards inclusivity wherever possible, but to always be genuine.

SECTION 4

SETTING UP YOUR ENRICHED
MARKETING STRATEGY

CHAPTER 15

MARKETING COMMUNICATION MILESTONES

'The aim of marketing is to know and understand the customer so well the product and services fits him and sells itself.' - Peter Drucker, father of management thinking

In the Grimms' classic fairy tale, Hansel and Gretel, a pair of unfortunate siblings are banished into an enchanted wood by their frustrated parents. As they walk together into the land of darkness and confusion (the woods, in this story), Hansel lays a trail of white pebbles in their wake so they can retrace their steps back to the land of light, their home.

Smart kids! They simply reverse-engineered their way home by following the path that had already been laid out for them.

Enriched Marketing works exactly the same way.

We're going to create a trail of marketing communication milestones which your clients will follow from their land of darkness and confusion, where they're consumed by their problem, to your island of light and joy, where you can make that problem go away with whatever it is you're selling to them.

Before we create that trail, it's important to understand the difference between sales and marketing, because they're not the same thing.

Marketing is the process of getting people across your bridge and into your business ecosystem. It brings them from the outside world to your point of sale. Marketing is an invitation to your island.

Sales is the process of asking for their money when they're standing on your doorstep at your point of sale. Sales is the act of asking them to buy something when they arrive.

In a brick-and-mortar shop, the marketing person would stand outside on the sidewalk with a big sign saying 'problem-free solutions inside', and the seller would be on the shop floor taking the customers' money.

Sales and marketing have completely different jobs to do, but every business in the world needs both, and the sales and marketing messages need to work together to grow your business.

Up until now, we've focused on building your island of light and joy, and crafting your perfect sales story. This chapter looks at what you need to say to people to keep them moving across your marketing bridge. These are your marketing communication milestones, or your breadcrumb trail.

The biggest difference between sales and marketing is the way people consume your messaging.

Sales communication is easy because it happens when people are looking to buy from you. It's relatively simple. You tell them how you can solve their problem, give them a price, and ask them to buy.

Marketing communication is a lot more complex, because marketing communication is designed to educate, inspire, or entertain people without directly asking them to buy something from you. People consume your marketing content in the background over a long period of time while they're crossing your bridge. Then if they like what they see while they're on your bridge, they step into your business ecosystem and ask what they can buy from you.

In a brick-and-mortar shop, they follow the marketer's sign onto the shop floor. In a digital shop, they follow the marketer's breadcrumb trail to land on your sales page.

Many businesses fail because they don't understand the difference between sales and marketing, or how the two work together, so they use upside-down thinking to chase the demand and lose out on making meaningful sales.

For the average business, the abridged workflow for creating a sales and marketing strategy often looks like this:

1. I want a business. What would I like to do with that?

2. This is what I want to do, so other people will love it too!

3. Let me make some demand for it: I'll invest in marketing myself on social media.

4. On no! Why is nobody coming to buy from me?

5. The market for this must be saturated. I need to stand out from the competition. Hmm. What's my USP?

6. I'll make a new social media strategy to show that I'm faster, better, and shinier.

7. Why is this still not working? It must be the algorithm that keeps changing.

8. Oh no, I need to close my business because I don't have any more money to spend on marketing and I have no customers to pay me.

This happens because the average business thinks that sales and marketing are the same thing, so they think only about how to market themselves to generate more leads.

Most businesses think about how to market the business before they think about how to sell their services, and I believe this is the top reason why so many businesses never reach their full potential.

This is important because it doesn't matter how many people you tell about your products and services if your sales story misses the mark.

Going back to our beetroot cupcakes and the high street versus bakery example, you can tell 1,000 people the wrong sales story and perhaps make one lucky sale, or you can tell ten people the right sales story and make ten sales.

It's cheaper and more efficient to tell the right sales story than it is to rely on guesswork in your marketing strategy.

Creating predictable revenue with Enriched Marketing is not

about how you create demand for your business, it's about saying the right thing to your ideal clients to inspire a successful sale. That starts with caring about who you sell to, and caring deeply for your dream clients.

Do you see how none of the eight phases of the average workflow above are about the customer?

This business will fail to sell with care because they've made a self-serving business without first thinking about the dream client's monkey brain. Having the wrong sales story will likely cause the marketing campaign to flop.

The monkey holds the purse. If you want to sell to the monkey, then you need to create a sales story that speaks to the monkey. When you figure out how to sell to the monkey, then your marketing strategy develops organically to keep that monkey brain interested.

MARKETING MAKES THE MONKEY REALISE THAT IT NEEDS TO BUY SOMETHING.

Let's take a quick recap of what we've done so far to reverse-engineer the dream client into our business ecosystem – where we can sell to them.

1. We identified how we can best help people with an Ikigai service or product.

2. We worked out who cares about getting that help.

3. We sought to understand *why* the solution really matters

to the people who care about getting our help.

4. We picked an archetype and found out how their monkey, reptilian, and everyday jackass brains make buying decisions.

5. We created an emotional map to outline which of their heartstrings should be pulled to entice the yes response in a basic sales pitch.

6. We created a brand personality to reflect the right purpose, mission and values that will appeal to the exact same client that we've written our sales pitch for.

7. We defined our unique mechanism for success in relation to the dream client's past failed attempts to solve their problem.

8. We made sales and about pages that reflects the dream client's values, to align us with them.

In contrast to the average sales and marketing strategy that most businesses use, this approach has set the business up to sell precisely the right thing to exactly the right person, by building the dream client's inherent psychological motivators into our sales pitch.

All we need to do now is lay a nice little trail of marketing communication milestones for the dream client to follow, and they will come to us to buy our stuff – because they want to!

Working backwards, much like Hansel and Gretel did, we'll start by understanding what a client who is ready to buy from you knows about your business, then we'll unpack that information into smaller pieces, which can be consumed one pebble at a time until they reach your door.

Hansel starts his trail of pebbles by setting out from home with a pocket full of stones. When Hansel and Gretel realise they've been abandoned in the woods, they find their way home by following their trail of pebbles back to their starting point.

We're going to do the same with your dream clients. We'll give them a trail of pebbles to follow, until they reach your door. Each pebble has specific information they need to absorb before they can take the next step. When they arrive in your business ecosystem, they will have received everything they need to know for the monkey to buy whatever it is you're selling.

We do it this way because of an important lesson that I learned selling photographs to the tune of 5 million dollars on luxury cruise ships – and because research has shown that autonomy matters in the psychology of persuasion.*

People only say yes when they believe it's their own decision. If they think you're trying to sell to them or push them into a decision they're not ready to make, then they'll just think you're sleazy, and that's when sales gets icky. If they're not ready to say yes, then the only possible answer, is no.

When the dream client arrives at your door with a pocket full of money, ready to pay for the opportunity to choose you, they must be there because they genuinely want to be there. Our marketing communication milestones build that desire, and guide people towards your point of sale.

---

* Cialdini, R.B (2008) Influence. 5th ed. Upper Saddle River, NJ: Pearson

THE MARKETING COMMUNICATION MILESTONES MATCH THE DREAM CLIENT'S CHANGING AWARENESS.

Consumer decision-making follows a set pattern which is based on the way most people learn, and is largely just logical.

People will first become aware of their problem. Next, they will research ways to solve it, then they'll evaluate alternative solutions. When they're happy with the information they have gathered, they will make their decision.

We'll give the dream client one milestone for each stage of awareness.

When they say yes to you, they will be ready to choose you of their own accord because they know what their problem is, and what your solution can do for them. They'll accept your solution is the best amongst various alternatives, and they'll know what to expect from the end result.

To get to this stage, they'll have had to make some key decisions and will have received key pieces of matching information to help them make those decisions. These nuggets of information are your marketing communication milestones. They're pieces of marketing content that people must receive in the right order to keep them moving towards your point of sale.

This is sometimes called 'pillar' content and refers to silos of information that can be drawn from to create your social media content.

The goal of this exercise is to spend an afternoon brainstorming as much as you can for each milestone using nice, easy bullet points, which can be used to spark ongoing ideas for content on demand as needed in the future.

I like to keep a Word document for each milestone (or pillar), but you can do this however it suits you best.

MILESTONE 1: KNOWLEDGE (AWARENESS)

At the start of the journey, the dream client either doesn't know what their problem is, or they don't know the solution exists.

The knowledge milestone is given to people with the lowest level of product awareness, so for this milestone, our goal is to regularly tell people what your product or service is, how it works, and why they need it until they build up an awareness of the problem and the solution.

In the case of our travel agent, the dream client may not recognise that they need help planning their holiday, or alternatively, they perhaps do know they need help with it, but don't know what a travel agent is or what travel agents can do to assist.

Before we can do anything else, we need to make sure that your future clients know what the problem is, what the solution looks like, and what you can physically do to assist them.

Using broad brushstrokes, brainstorm a few quick points to describe what your client's problem is, and what your Ikigai service does to remedy it. You don't need to do this with intricate detail, you're just looking to capture the essence of what people need to know about your business, your service, and your industry. in general.

For our travel agent, we might say:

- People struggle to make their own travel arrangements because they don't know what they don't know, so they don't know what to look for when choosing a hotel.

- Travel agents provide advice about where to go and which hotels to choose, so you can get the best experience.

- Travel agents help people to make travel arrangements by booking hotels on their behalf.

- Travel agents have access to rates, availability, and special offers, so you can get everything you need in one place without getting confused.

Keep it simple. What does a business with your Ikigai service do?

MILESTONE 2: BELIEF (RESEARCH)

The belief milestone is the research phase.

Why do people stand in long lines, sometimes for hours, waiting to ride a scary rollercoaster that promises to be deeply uncomfortable?

It's because the long line usually runs alongside the exit gate.

People waiting their turn to scare themselves see others coming back from the experience with glee on their smiling faces. Despite all evidence to the contrary, people believe that if others enjoy it, they will too, so they wait in line for hours thinking it will be worth it.

If people came off the ride white-faced and covered in puke, no one would go on the ride, and the multimillion-dollar rollercoaster industry would promptly go bankrupt.

We are all sheep. Beautiful, predictable sheep that can be guided and steered in any direction you choose, as long as you say the right thing at the right time to make us believe we *want* to follow you from the land of darkness and confusion straight to your waiting door.

The belief milestone is for people who have solid problem awareness and know how you can help. They are now evaluating your credibility and deciding if your solution is right for them. They know you offer a scary rollercoaster, so they're looking at your safety standards and checking that other people are coming off the ride with smiles.

This game-changing milestone builds trust in your brand and product. It's what makes your solution believable to the dream client.

WHAT DO PEOPLE NEED TO SEE AND BELIEVE BEFORE THEY WILL TRUST YOU?

1. SCIENTIFIC PROOF

Scientific proof is about demonstrating the safety of your system. If you're in the business of building rollercoasters, then why is yours trustworthy?

For our travel agent, we can show that the business is regulated by an external body, or insured by a payment protection scheme. If you have a product that uses a known system, you'll show some kind of proof that the secret ingredient works. Build credibility by referencing published research or your own data.

What can you show that highlights your credentials? What have you learned or earned that makes you an industry authority?

2. SOCIAL PROOF

Social proof is about highlighting who else uses your services, and why they like you.

There are two ways you can show your future clients why other people want your product, and you should ideally use both.

The first way is to show what others think of you. If you're in the rollercoaster business, you can show social proof by positioning your waiting clients alongside those returning with smiles on their faces.

For our travel agent, we can show social proof by gathering testimonials and displaying online reviews on the website.

The second way is to show that other people want what you

offer. This demonstrates demand and makes your product feel exclusive to those who are in the know about how good you really are.

The rollercoaster industry demonstrates demand-based social proof perfectly. If people wish to ride a rollercoaster, they must first wait in line, sometimes for hours, before they can experience 67 seconds of heart-stopping fear. The rollercoaster only accepts a handful of people for each ride, so naturally, that makes everybody want a seat in the car, even if they have to stand in the blazing-hot sun and wait for it.

Many people who ride rollercoasters only do it because everybody else says they should. This is social proof in action.

Social proof is much the same as the peer pressure people feel when they're deciding whether or not to go on a rollercoaster they don't want to ride. If everybody else is doing it, people believe they should be doing it too.

Social proof is a collection of opinions gathered from others. Exclusivity is the perception that using your service makes people feel ultra-special.

If you can prove both sides of this evaluation process, then you have a winner. The more proof you can provide, and the more specific that proof is, the easier it becomes to believe in your brand, and the more likely it is that the dream client's research will lead to your business.

Importantly, scientific and social proof work together in tandem, so you need to provide some information from *both* sets of proof – social proof (what others say), and scientific proof (what the known results say).

Again, keep this brainstorming quite broad. You're just looking for the 'a-ha' moment when your dream client sees your Ikigai solution is possible, so they can start to investigate whether or not your business is right for them.

For our travel agent, the dream client needs to believe:

- Holidays are better when somebody who knows how to find the best hotels helps plan the itinerary. (Social)

- Other people use travel agents to plan holidays. (Social)

- This travel agent has a good reputation with other happy clients. (Social)

- This travel agent can back up their claims with the right licences and insurance plans to guarantee my safety. (Scientific)

Returning to the rollercoaster analogy, if someone still thinks rollercoasters are not for them after seeing both social and scientific proof, then you'd need to return them to the previous milestone – the knowledge milestone – and educate them on why they want to ride a rollercoaster at all. You need them to buy into the concept of rollercoasters before asking them to join the waiting line of people who are looking at the smiling faces of others coming off the ride.

One milestone must come before the other.

What do people need to fundamentally believe before they will be open to the idea of your Ikigai service?

Keep it simple. What are people saying, and what do you have that can back up your claims?

Milestone 3: Readiness (evaluation)

The readiness milestone relates to how your dream client has previously tried to resolve their pain in the past.

Oftentimes, people don't even know what their primary pain is. But if you pick apart their frustrations, then you'll nearly always find they have tried to resolve their pain in multiple ways without success, whether they're aware of it or not.

What do your dream clients need to have learned from past failures before they will open themselves to something new?

In the weight-loss example, people who chose Noom had previously tried to eat a variety of healthy diets. This failed because the diets didn't address the underlying emotional issues.

What makes your dream clients ready to accept your unique mechanism for delivering the results they want?

Make a list of everything your dream clients might have tried in the past, then think about why this doesn't work, and why your way of doing it is better.

For our travel agent, we might say:

- **They booked a hotel on a comparison site.** This didn't work because the hotel was in the wrong location for the experience they wanted. I have access to an industry map that shows which locations offer different types of experiences.

- **They booked via an unlicensed travel agent.** This didn't work because when there were travel restrictions in place, the hotel refused to give their money back. I have a regulated licence which guarantees they will get their money back if they can't travel due to travel restrictions.

- **They tried to book directly with the hotel.** This didn't work because the hotel couldn't offer airport transfers, so they didn't know how to get there. I book a hotel package, so they don't need to worry about transportation.

Keep it simple. What didn't work out for them last time that highlights the benefit of choosing you this time?

MILESTONE 4: RESULT (DECISION)

Your result milestone speaks directly to the highest level of market awareness.

By the time people are asking questions about specific results, they already know what your product or service does, and believe you are trustworthy. They also recognise they need something that's fundamentally different to what they've tried before if they're going to solve the right problem to get rid of their underlying pain.

At this stage of the buying process, your dream clients are looking for reasons to say yes! They *want* you to be the right choice, and they're looking for every possible reason to allow themselves to say yes. This is your chance to show off your unique mechanism and the results you can achieve with it, which inspires their monkey brain to make the purchase.

When your prospects reach this part of your bridge, they're ready to step onto your island of light and joy to buy whatever it is you've got. You need only present your sales pitch, and the client with the right archetype's monkey brain will buy into it without hesitation.

But – and this is a big but – they will only do that provided they have already been given everything else they need in the previous three phases of knowledge, belief, and readiness to make their yes decision. The monkey needs to know the reptile will benefit from the purchase.

For the result milestone, we want to show people what a world without their problem looks like, using the right style of language that resonates with the dream client. This is your 4-point story taken from the emotional map.

For our travel agent's innocent archetype, we wrote:

'We help ambitious people to book luxury hotels, so you can take a break to enjoy life's little moments without hitting burnout.'

Once you have your marketing communication milestones fully brainstormed, you'll want to go back into your basic sales page and pad it out using the same structure we created previously.

Add details to each section, and make sure that you're telling people everything they need to hear before they will say yes. To recap, our sales page has nine steps:

1. Headline

2. Introduction

3. Scientific proof

4. Offer details

5. Social proof

6. Add value

7. Reverse risk

8. Call to action

9. Urgency or scarcity

The details must flow in this order, but you can now insert the extra information you've gathered for your marketing communication milestones into your sales page as follows:

1. Headline (call out the dream client)

2. Introduction (knowledge milestone)

3. Scientific proof (belief milestone part one)

4. Offer details (readiness milestone)

5. Social proof (belief milestone part two)

6. Add value (result milestone)

7. Reverse risk (result milestone)

8. Call to action (the big red sales button)

9. Urgency or scarcity (the deadline or the exclusivity)

Do you see how the marketing communication milestones match the sales pitch? We do this so that people know what to expect when they get to your point of sale.

The marketing message does the pre-selling. It warms people up for what you have for sale and makes them hungry for it. The sales page closes the deal.

USE YOUR MARKETING COMMUNICATION MILESTONES TO GENERATE FOOTFALL FOR YOUR BUSINESS.

When creating your marketing communication milestones, try to use broad brushstroke thinking to keep it loose. We just need to paint a big enough picture, so the dream client gains enough awareness to progress to the next level.

Hansel didn't explain the difference between every white pebble laid on his trail. He just put them down where they needed to be, and Gretel followed them home.

All you need to do is drop a selection of thoughtfully arranged marketing communication milestones into the correct parts of your ongoing marketing campaigns, and the dream client will happily follow you from their island of darkness and confusion straight to your open door.

These four milestones become your pillars for creating marketing content.

The idea is to create a single document for each milestone where you can gather your thoughts in depth about what people need to know at each stage of the process. Keep these documents to hand. You can use them to inspire ideas for your organic content marketing campaigns.

You want to give your dream clients information taken from your milestone pillars at the right times to match their current level of awareness, and move them a step closer to using your service. This can be done in real conversations, in social media posts, in podcasts, or even via email as appropriate for your business.

Simply match your dream client's existing level of awareness to your marketing when you start talking to them wherever they're at, and the conversation will move them from one milestone to the next until they say yes.

If your target audience has zero awareness, show them the knowledge milestone first. If they're looking for trust, show the belief milestone. When people are stuck in a pattern of bad outcomes, show them the readiness milestone. If your target audience already has a high level of awareness, then start with the result and act fast to close the sale!

You can string these milestones together in your everyday marketing by following a basic funnel format that links social media to your point of sale.

There are lots of different ways to do it and that's enough to fill another book, but here's one easy way to use these milestones in your marketing strategy.

Step 1 – Social media post (knowledge, for problem awareness)

Make a social media post that draws from the knowledge milestone. Our travel agent might make a post about how difficult it can be to choose the right hotel when you don't know what you don't know.

This post should direct people to a longer, more informative article, perhaps on your blog, podcast, or LinkedIn newsletter.

Step 2 – Long-form article (belief, for research)

Provide a complete story that shows you know your stuff! Answer a single common question in depth, and make sure it gives both social and scientific proof to win people's trust in your ability to help.

This longer piece of content should direct people to your sales page on your website.

Step 3 – Website sales page (readiness, for evaluation)

Show people an irresistible sales page that demonstrates why your solution is fundamentally different to everything that's failed before. Win them over with your 4-point story that's based on their archetype-driven emotional map.

Step 4 – Call to action (result, for their decision)

Be very clear about the next step with an obvious button that asks them to buy from you!

Once you have completed your four pillar documents – knowledge, belief, readiness, and result – they will serve as inspiration and help create content ideas for your long-term content-marketing strategy.

There are hundreds of different ways you can present your content, and you'll need to give content from all of your milestones multiple times to gain traction, but persevere.

The more people see your consistent messaging in their peripheral vision online, the more familiar you'll become, and the closer they will move towards your business.

Be consistent. Post regularly, and take the time to engage with people who interact with you to develop your relationship until they're ready to buy from you.

LIKE FROGS ON A LILY PAD

Another nice way to look at the marketing communication milestones is to think about the way a frog crosses a pond filled with lily pads. It hops from one pad to the next, until it gets to the other side.

Your marketing communication milestones are the lily pads, and your dream clients are the frogs.

First, they jump to the knowledge lily pad to discover what their problem is and how to solve it. Next, they jump to the belief lily pad to research their options. Thirdly, they jump to the readiness lily pad to evaluate if you're right for them.

By the time our frogs get to the fourth lily pad, where you ask them to say yes to your stuff, they're already closer to your side of the pond than they are to the place they started from.

It's much easier for a frog to hop from the fourth lily pad into your business ecosystem than it is to go back and start again in somebody else's pond.

A 5-MINUTE CHALLENGE

Answer the below questions without thinking too hard about the answers. Give yourself a maximum of 1 minute per question, and write your answers down.

1. What do you do?

2. Why are you qualified to do that?

3. Why do people like you?

4. Why do people struggle to solve the thing you solve?

5. Who is your target client?

How have your answers changed from the answers you wrote down when you started reading this book?

CHAPTER 16

A BASKET OF WORDS

'Language is the road map of a culture.
It tells you where its people come from and where
they are going.'- Rita Mae Brown, Rubyfruit Jungle

Your brand language is a road map that defines how you speak to and engage with your audience at every touch point. Consider, for example, the difference between teaching a group of teenage actors how to perform on stage, and delivering a talk on climate change to leaders of the United Nations.

In the first setting, we'll speak with energy and enthusiasm to create a sense of fun and instil confidence. In the second setting, we'll talk with gravitas and passion to try to provoke positive change.

If we talk to the teenagers with the voice of fear, then they would likely fail as actors. Similarly, if we give a fun and bubbly speech about climate change, then we will likely struggle to get world leaders to take it seriously.

Your brand language determines how you speak to your intended audience.

Now, many copywriters and brand storytellers will tell you that the best way to create a brand language for your audience is to spend time in the places where they spend time, so you can learn the types of words they use and bring them into your brand language.

This is partially true. You do need to bring a language that your dream client can relate to into your copywriting and brand story, but you don't need to spend countless hours trying to learn how to speak *like* them.

In fact, trying to speak precisely like the people who hang out in your audience hot spots, like Facebook groups or LinkedIn feeds, is pretty much impossible because these audiences are filled with individuals, and every individual uses their own choice of words.

For example, if you spend time around Gen Z, they may use trendy words like 'fam' and 'YOLO'.* But not all Gen Zs use these words, and your audience may not only consist of Gen Zs.

A better way to do it is to create language that's archetype-specific, not 'group of people in my collective audience'-specific. In other words, we want to tap into words that people with our dream client's archetype will understand, rather than the types of words that people in our audience like using today.

---

* Short for 'family' and 'you only live once.'

Luckily, you've already done the work. Your brand language should be guided by your overarching brand personality, which we determined from your brand's archetype. The overarching brand personalities are competent, sincere, rugged, excited, and sophisticated.

These different brand personalities can resonate with a whole range of different people – regardless of their age, gender, profession and so on. So you don't need to box yourself in trying to speak to one particular demographic. What matters is how you deliver your message, and how that message makes your dream client feel.

Remember, people don't buy goods or services. They buy the experience you create for them when they interact with your brand. If they like what you say and how you say it, then they say yes to whatever it is you're selling.

The trick to creating incredible customer experiences is to create a brand language that's so comfortable for the dream client to hear, that it becomes nearly impossible to turn their attention away from you.

WE CAN CHANGE THE WAY PEOPLE FEEL JUST BY CHANGING THEIR EXPERIENCE.

Every touchpoint with your future customers contributes to their overall experience, even if the effect is not immediately seen. In my cruise-ship photography days, I learned the hard way that guests who were chased around the ship for a picture seldom said yes.

One evening, I was standing next to my empty studio asking the 100th guest to stop for a picture without success, when the pianist, Bruce, dropped in for a chat.

"You need to smudge the people," he said. "Make them want to stop for a chat, then take their picture before they leave."

From that moment onwards, I never again asked for a photo without first becoming genuinely curious about the people I was pitching to. When one person stops to chat, they all do. Soon I had 20 people standing in line waiting to have their portrait taken, and became the most popular studio night after night.

Changing the experience the guests had in my studio changed the way they felt about having their picture taken. Instead of making it about me and my photos, I made it about them and their stunning evening outfits.

Letting people feel good about wearing a formal dress to dinner meant they were happy to embrace having their pictures taken, where they had previously just rushed past the studio feeling uncomfortable with idea of photography, scared I would ask them to stop with my large lens and fancy lights.

Experiences are the subtle, intangible feelings we create for others, and they're incredibly powerful when used correctly. We can control these experiences by tweaking the style of language we use to communicate with potential clients. This is your brand language.

Brand language is also sometimes called your brand tone of voice. It's responsible for the feeling or general experience your story creates when we read your brand messaging.

Creating a brand language starts with a basket of words that are used as building blocks for all your brand messaging in every format. These words collectively represent who you are, who you serve, what you value, and why that matters.

How to brainstorm your brand words

Your basket of words should have around 30 to 50 words or phrases that are easy to remember, simple to use, and perfectly aligned with your brand story. The best way to come up with them is to brainstorm at least a hundred words or phrases, then choose the ones you're most comfortable using.

The good news is that we already have a solid starting point.

All you need is a few trigger words. I'll use the travel agent example again here to show you where the words have come from, and where you can find them in your workings. Your list of starting words and phrases is as follows:

- Your archetype (see chapter 7): **innocent**

- Your archetype's subgroup's core need: **independent**

- Your archetype's reptilian need: **feel safe**

- Your archetype's monkey need: **blissful moments**

- Your dream client's 'hope' word (see chapter 8): **luxury**

- Your dream client's goal: **take a break**

- Your dream client's 'desire' words: **enjoy life's little moments**

- Your overarching brand personality (see chapter 12): **sincerity**

- Your five brand values: **simplicity, purity, kindness, compassion, generosity**

- Your five personality styles: **relaxed, approachable, friendly, warm, open**

Use this as a starting point to create a list of powerful words that are relevant to your business. You could use a thesaurus or AI chatbot to generate similar words to the ones above.

For our travel agent, we may come up with a basket of 50 brand words that look a bit like this:

Innocent. Independent. Feel. Safety. Bliss. Moments. Sincere. Simple. Pure. Kind. Compassionate. Generous. Relaxing. Approachable. Friendly. Warmth. Open. Luxurious. Restful. Sweet. Gentle. Soft. Delicate. Comfortable. Secure. Delightful. Experience. Dream. Serene. Authentic. Trusted. Paradise. Playful. Happy. Uncomplicated. Space. Easy. Heartfelt. Organic. Stress-free. Refreshing. Rejuvenating. Pristine. Light. Laid-back. Barefoot. Thoughtful. Idyllic. Delightful. Welcoming.

Once you have your basket of words, go back into your sales and about pages and scatter them into your story to add depth.

When you've finished creating any new content for your business, always go back and sprinkle words from your basket of words into your content. You can use these words for ads and social media, blogs, website content, sales proposals, voiceover scripts, and anything else you choose. Use them for hashtags and headlines too.

Your basket of words should pepper all interactions with your current and future clients, so use them to describe yourself at every opportunity. This lets you create a tone of voice that's always on brand and only speaks to your dream clients. Over time, your business will become laser-focused on *only* the right types of people who are a perfect fit for your business.

The dead-weight leads who just don't get it will fall away naturally, so your 'sorry, I'm not able to help with that' responses will become a distant memory as your business grows. In the Enriched Marketing future, every new lead should bring both money and joy into your business.

The better you get at using your basket of words to guide and shape the experiences you create for your clients, the stronger your brand will be, and the easier it will be to stand out to the clients you most want to attract into your business ecosystem.

Top Tip! Pick a small selection of words from your basket for conversational use. When speaking about your business in person, use these words and watch your dream clients' eyes start to twinkle.

SECTION 5

FINDING BOTH MONEY AND JOY IN YOUR BUSINESS

CHAPTER 17

THREE OFFERS THAT MAKE MONEY!

'I feel that luck is preparation meeting opportunity.' - Oprah Winfrey, American talk-show host

As enriched marketers, our only goal is to create the perception of magic, and to pull the right triggers to make impossible scenarios feel wholly achievable.

In reverse-engineered marketing, we first figure out what our dream clients need us to be, then we become the brand that answers *precisely* to that need, for the dream client only.

We create empathy by showing that we truly understand their experience, and we build likeability by showing the dream client that we're the same as them through the experiences we create for them at every touchpoint.

Enriched Marketing works because we're 'mirroring' the dream client at every step on their journey towards our business, giving them a thoughtful trail of marketing communication milestones that lead them away from their place of confusion straight to your open door.

In psychology, mirroring happens when we intentionally copy someone to get them to like us. It's also used as an important tool for learning and development. Colloquially, mirroring is known as 'monkey see, monkey do', or 'see one, do one, teach one'.

When we watch somebody else experience something, our human capacity for empathy means the brain can form similar neural connections to those we would form if we experienced it ourselves.

Our reverse-engineered dream clients see something of themselves in our brand story, and recognise that we can solve their problems, so they make neural connections that link their problem to our solution in their brains. Powerful stuff!

All we need to do now is put the right offers in front of them, and they'll say yes. But what is the best offer?

THE BEST OFFERS MAKE YOUR BUSINESS EFFICIENT, PROFITABLE, AND VALUABLE TO YOUR DREAM CLIENTS.

Your offers must bring both money and joy into your business. They should deliver value to your dream clients, and they should actively work towards freeing up your time to live a balanced, more rewarding life. After all, isn't that why you reached up and took your dream of running your own business into your hands?

Every business should have a collection of offers that work together to keep people loyal, generate more customers, and scale profits without needing additional resources.

The best offers work like nesting dolls. Nesting dolls are three dolls which fit one inside the other to create three layers.

Your inner nesting doll – the premium offer

At the top end of what you do, you'll have a premium offer that generates a high level of income from a small pool of clients. This is usually an exclusive or one-to-one offer where the client gets a comprehensive service on a private basis for a higher fee.

For example, if you're a coaching business or a creative service, you might offer a comprehensive done-for-you package with a full suite of service inclusions and personal support that's delivered one-to-one.

The premium offer is what increases your profitability, because it increases the average spend per client. Let's say you advertise your premium offer to a hundred people and three of them buy it. If your premium offer is 25k then a hundred people will generate 75k, and will have an average order value of $750.

If your premium offer is only 1k, and you generate three sales for every hundred people you advertise to, then those three sales will generate just 3k, and your average order value will be $30.

To make your business profitable, you need to have a high-value premium offer that can be sold to a handful of clients. This is how you get to pick and choose only the best clients who always bring money and joy into running your business.

Your middle nesting doll — the growth offer

In the middle, you'll have a growth offer that delivers the same result as your premium offer, but to a larger pool of clients. This is achieved either by using an automated delivery system, or a one-to-many format.

Growth offers are usually either sold on a continuity pricing system where people pay a monthly membership, as an event with many seats for sale, or as pre-made content that's created once and sold on repeat.

For example, if you're a coaching business or a creative service, you may have a subscription model where people can access all of your content via an app or YouTube channel for a low monthly fee.

Alternatively, you might run a live event or seminar where people can buy tickets to access your service in a group format. Finally, you may have a digital course they can purchase once and complete at home without you being physically present to deliver the results.

The middle offer is what grows your revenue because you don't need to physically be involved in delivering the outcome for every customer. If you make your course and deliver it to one person for 1k, then you will make 1k every time you deliver a live course. To make 30k, you would need to deliver the same course 30 times.

If you deliver the same content once to a hundred people at a group event, and charge just $300 for it, then you will make 30k and your offer will be viewed as valuable to people who have smaller budgets. If you can pre-record the event and sell it digitally to a thousand people, then you will make 300k from the same content.

Growth offers make your business more efficient.

With growth offers, the number of new clients you can handle becomes limitless if you can deliver the same service to an infinite number of people without upping your resources.

This is how you scale profit, so you'll want to be thinking about how you can develop your one-to-many services from the outset.

Your outer nesting doll – the attraction offer

The attraction offer is a low-cost offer that gets people through the door and turns them into paying customers, even if they only buy a very small service for a very small fee.

Attraction offers are important because the easiest person to sell a high-value service to is an existing customer. People who buy your attraction offers are prime prospects to later move on to a growth or a premium offer.

But there's a catch to this. Your attraction offer must be a component of your premium service, just like your growth offer must deliver the same result as your premium service with less exclusivity for a lower fee.

For example, if you're a coaching business you might create a short, low-cost workshop that demonstrates one principle from your growth offer. You'll then show the growth offer to people who liked the attraction offer, and if that goes well, you'll later move the same client from your growth offer into your premium offer.

Your attraction offer fills your business with a steady flow of people who are pre-conditioned to buy your high-end offers, because they already have a relationship with you.

If your attraction offer has no relevance to your premium offer, which should be your ultimate Ikigai service, then you will inadvertently create a reactive structure where the people coming through your door for the low-cost offers are not suitable for your most profitable services.

These three offers are a formidable combination of products and services, which together, bring both money and joy into your business – as long as they're always working towards the same goal, which is to pull people into your most profitable premium offer.

Now, you might be sitting here thinking, that's great for coaching businesses and for people in creative services, but my business is a physical service. This won't work!

Some industries are indeed easier to create these three offers for than others are, but I believe that's just a mindset. Let's look at these offers again in a slightly different way.

Our goal is to use information to sell your Ikigai service

or product. We're going to achieve that by giving people the information they need, then showing them where they can buy extra value, until they realise that what they really want is your Ikigai offer – your premium offer.

Your attraction offer's only job is to get a potential paying client's foot in the door. This is sometimes called a lead magnet or a tripwire. It's usually something cheap and cheerful, and it's very often free. Its purpose is to give people a taste of what to expect if they venture further into your business ecosystem.

Let's say your dream client has crossed your brand-story bridge from their island of darkness and confusion to your island of light and joy, and they're standing at the entrance to your business ecosystem. You might like to offer them a welcome drink before you start selling your premium offer.

THE ATTRACTION OFFER IS YOUR WELCOME DRINK.

As Bruce the pianist so rightfully pointed out, you want to 'smudge the people'* before you jump in with an offer for your most expensive package.

If you're selling physical products, this might include giving away a free sample or creating a small taster pack of whatever it is you have. Starter kits work well as attraction offers because

---

* According to Bruce, 'smudging the people' is the opposite of a time-old idiom. It's rubbing people up the right way before pitching your services, so they'll like you.

they let people try before they buy without too much investment.

If you're selling services (including software), then a free trial or an information product like a short course or weekend workshop works well. You may like to host a webinar or run a social media group to educate people about how they can get the most value out of whatever it is you do.

Our travel agent might host a talk on where to travel at different times of year, or where to go for particular types of trips like honeymoons or retirement years abroad. An interior decorator might make a booklet on choosing the right colours for every room.

The attraction offer should deliver exceptional value with genuine answers to your dream clients' burning questions. This is key, because the more you can show people what you know about your area of expertise, the more likely it is that they'll trust you to do a good job. Don't hold back!

THE GROWTH OFFER IS AN INVITATION FOR YOUR DREAM CLIENTS TO STICK AROUND AND GET COMFORTABLE IN YOUR BUSINESS ECO-SYSTEM.

Once people have crossed your brand-story bridge and enjoyed a delicious welcome drink in the form of your attraction offer, the next step is to keep them happy, so they choose to stay.

The goal of the growth offer is to create revenue continuity. You want people to buy into your business with a regular, recurring payment. This gives your business some predictable income, but more importantly, keeps your clients emotionally invested.

A good way to look at this is to consider a membership at a local health club. A monthly membership means you can go to the spa whenever you want to use the facilities, and as part of your membership, you get to be part of the club of people who are members.

This creates a sense of exclusivity. Even if you hardly ever go to the spa or use the facilities, and even if it would be a lot cheaper to just buy a spa day once a year if you want one, it still feels nice to be in the club. That feeling of being part of the community creates consistent revenue for the health club, and makes cancelling your membership very difficult.

Growth offers follow the same principle.

How can you deliver ongoing value to your clients in exchange for a regular payment that makes the client feel special for being part of the club?

Coaches and creatives might offer access to all of their content for a small monthly fee. If you sell products, you might have a monthly box of goodies. If you sell software or professional services, then you may choose to offer a monthly retainer with fixed inclusions.

Our travel agent might create a paid-for newsletter that highlights all the tricks and tips for getting the best value out of staying at luxury hotels. A wellness coach might create a box of small feel-good gifts to send to clients each month. The value in the information (or service) received fetches a predictable fee that people are happy to pay for.

THE PREMIUM OFFER IS WHAT YOU DO BEST FOR YOUR DREAM CLIENTS – YOUR IKIGAI OFFER.

When people are comfortable in your business ecosystem and want more of whatever it is you've got, then it's very easy to ask if they want your premium service. Most will say yes because it makes sense to buy the next product from you instead of your competition.

Going back to our health spa example, the membership is just to keep you comfortable. While you're at the spa, there's a very good chance that you'll be offered a massage or a facial, and when you're presented with this easy upgrade it becomes effortless to add a nice massage to your day out. You're already there, primed for more, so why not?

Think about this from the spa's perspective for a moment. It's far more efficient and profitable to sell occasional massages to people who already pay a monthly spa membership fee than it is to upsell a day spa pass to people who book a once-off massage. The growth offer sells the premium offer to boost revenue, but the regular income comes from the members.

If you think carefully about what you do, you'll find that it's very easy to create these three types of offers for your business, regardless of your niche or industry.

Once you have them in place, then you can go back to your basic sales page structure (developed in Chapter 9), and tailor it for each of your three offers, making one additional sales page for each offer.

Remember, the basic sales page structure looks like this:

1. Headline (call out the dream client)

2. Introduction (knowledge milestone)

3. Scientific proof (belief milestone part one)

4. Offer details (readiness milestone)

5. Social proof (belief milestone part two)

6. Add value (result milestone)

7. Reverse risk (result milestone)

8. Call to action (the big red sales button)

9. Urgency of scarcity (the deadline)

These three new sales pages, which use the exact same development process for the same archetype, written in the same brand language as your main sales page, will become your product or service pages on your website.

Top Tip! Don't forget to sprinkle in some words from your brand's basket of words to capture the perfect tone of voice!

Interestingly, your offers might not always flow in the same sequence. For example, someone could buy into your attraction offer then purchase your premium offer straight away. These clients might be offered a more exclusive membership area with a customer support retainer at the end of the service to ensure continuity. Others may come straight to your growth offer and just stay there without purchasing your attraction or premium offer.

That's all ok. The three offers work together to attract warm leads, generate continuous income, and sell your Ikigai service. The revenue diversity creates resilience for enduring success.

Likewise, your service pages may not all appeal to exactly the same archetype. Each offer will have a specific dream client, and should be looked at independently using the process in this book. The deep psychological need should be the same – control, independence, recognition, or social belonging – but people who buy into different offers may have a slightly different driving force for choosing them.

I recently worked with a business where the main service has three very different avenues. We created an innocent brand, but one of the services was for an innocent archetype, one for a sage, and the other for the explorer.

All three services solve the same problem, which is how someone can find their independence, but one service solves it through escapism (explorer), one through learning (sage), and the other through finding life's sweet spot (innocent).

This is ok too: as long as the overarching brand story targets the strongest archetype, you can tailor individual services to suit similar archetypes. As long as you work through the full process for each product or service, and follow the steps with your main archetype in mind, then it will all work out just the way it should.

CHAPTER 18

THE POWER OF DATA

'We see our customers as invited guests to a party, and we are the hosts. It's our job every day to make every important aspect of the customer experience a little bit better.' - Jeff Bezos, founder of Amazon

Now that you've figured out who your dream client is, how to harness their deepest desires, and how to design them into your business, it's time to get them involved in refining your business.

Feedback is one of the most valuable ways you can measure what's working, and what's not. Throughout this process we've used principles and frameworks to create an experience-driven best guess into what our business is about, but that's not enough.

You need to continually assess and sharpen what you do to please your clients. The quest to always be focused on what the right customers want is what differentiates successful brands from mediocre businesses.

Customer feedback and active sales data are the secret sauce.

Actively ask people why they like you. Find out what you're really like to work with. Ask open questions and create a safe space for people to share their honest insights.

Also, ask people why they don't buy from you. If you lose a sale, find out why. Ask where you missed the mark, and make sure you know *why* you failed.

Finally, keep track of measurable conversion rates and test variations against each other. This is called A/B testing, and the goal is simply to create two version of the same thing with a subtle difference to see which one converts better.

You might switch a word in your heading, or use a different colour on your button. If the conversion rates go up, keep the change and test something else. If the conversion rates go down, lose the change and try again.

This is a bit like adding fresh décor to your home.

It's rare to give a room at home a full makeover all at once, but you might start small. Perhaps you'll paint the walls blue and see how you like them. If they're better than the previous colour, you might introduce some new cushions. If you like them, you might change the artwork. If you preferred the previous artwork, you can always just put the old picture back on the wall to reverse the change.

When we change everything all at once it's hard to pinpoint what works, and why. If you switch the wall colour, cushions and artwork on the same day, you'll know something isn't working, but you won't know if it's the colour of the walls, the shape of the cushions, or the new piece of art.

Gathering data for your brand story is about starting with your best attempt at the perfect story, which we've developed in this book, then making small tweaks to one detail at a time until you optimise your conversion rates for every element of your business.

Ask for feedback at every possible opportunity, and listen to the data wherever you find it.

In 1994, an investment banker quit his job, moved to Seattle, and started an online bookshop from the depths of his garage. People didn't buy much online in the 1990s, so most people thought he was beating to his own drum.

His business idea solved a simple problem: the limitations of choice.

In 1994, Jeff Bezos understood that physical bookshops were limited by how many different books they could stock at any one time, so customers either had to choose from what was available, or they had to wait a long time for a custom order.

Amazon's unique mechanism to solve this problem was to make all books available at the touch of a button. By the time brick-and-mortar bookstores like Barnes & Noble caught on to the concept of online shopping, Amazon had already changed the game.

In its early days, Jeff Bezos asked people why they liked Amazon. His existing customers told him that the variety of choice available was a huge positive, so he widened this further to include more choice in other products beyond just books.

Books, music and more…

If Amazon was to make a mark in the changing world of e-commerce, then Jeff Bezos needed to attract people who wanted everything they could possibly think of at the touch of a button.

Which types of people care about having everything they could ever want? Those who want to feel like a kid in a candy store!

Amazon created a sales campaign for adults who want to rediscover the joys of childhood. These are people who like fun, and fall into the jester archetype.

He created the ultimate Ikigai product, called 'EMAHTSKCBLVDT'. This is an acronym for a wide range of product categories covering everything from electronics, music and books to toys, beauty, and kitchenware.*

In 1999, Amazon launched a televised Christmas ad with a powerful overarching theme:

'Feel like a kid again, with the greatest selection of toys online!'

It worked perfectly! EMAHTSKCBLVDT has held its position as one of the world's most successful product collections for over 20 years, and at the time of writing this book, Jeff Bezos is worth a cool $165.7 billion.

Amazon's global success is a direct result of reverse-engineering the dream client – an adult version of the kid in a candy store – then asking them some pertinent questions:

---

* EMAHTSKCBLVDT is short for 'Electronics, Music, Auctions, Health and Beauty, Tools, Software, Kitchen, Cameras, Books, Lawn and Patio, Video Games, DVD, Toys.'

- Why do you like us?

- How can we make you like us even more?

Look at your data every day. You can do this by measuring clicks and interactions with your online content, and by analysing patterns in your existing client base. You'll also want to measure where people drop out of your business ecosystem, so you can understand why you lost them.

Pay attention to where people find you, and how they come to know about you. When they arrive, ask them how they got there. When they're happily part of your ecosystem, ask them what they like about being there. When they leave, ask them why they're no longer interested.

Follow the trends to see what people respond well to, and tweak your offers until you have everything just right. Then look at the data again. Tweak again.

In my early days as a cruise ship photographer, we had the privilege of doing this in real life. Sometimes, we could print the pictures and make no sales at all, then reprint the same pictures again the next day using a slightly different display and make record sales – from the exact same photos, of the exact same people!

Marketing is a science and an art.

There are no shortcuts or fast answers: you need to do the work, and if something is not working, rework it until it is. If your dream client turns out to be someone else, find out why. Harness your curiosity to unpack everything you can find about what resonates with your audience, and what doesn't.

When you know why something is successful, do more of the same.

If something keeps letting you down, find out why. Ask people why they don't like it. Look at the people who nearly became your clients, then see who they chose instead, and find out why.

Once you know why something is unsuccessful, do less of the same. Eventually, you'll iron out all the kinks in your client experience, and all those perfect clients who recognise themselves in you will follow your breadcrumb trail out of the land of darkness, straight to your open door.

CHAPTER 19

THE SECRET INGREDIENT

'Humility is not thinking less of yourself, it's thinking of yourself less.' - Rick Warren, *The Purpose-Driven Life*

O ver the course of my career, I've had the privilege of working closely with more than a few millionaires. What's struck me about all of my wealthiest clients is how grounded they are. They ask thought-provoking questions, listen to the answers, and make key decisions based on that.

Sales, service, and stories all share a common property. They rely on actively listening to convey the right message.

Enriched Marketing is about putting your clients first, listening to what they need, and then building a responsive brand that serves that need with the secret ingredient: humility.

It's not about you – it's about them.

Marketing fails when businesses put themselves first, and the customers second. If you make it about you, your customers will choose a brand that does put them first.

Success in brand storytelling doesn't come from throwing money at the problem, nor does it come from shouting your name from the rooftops with endless content on every platform you can find. Success comes from listening to what people want to hear, then telling them the right story.

The better you get at putting your ego aside to actively listen to what people and data tell you, the faster your route to success will be. The more you remove yourself from your story, your desires, and your reason for being in business, the more people start paying attention to you, because you start talking about the only things that really matter in business – your clients, and their needs.

Without clients, running a business is meaningless.

Ask people why they buy from you. Ask them why they don't. Ask what they really need, then give them that. Ask who they are, then show them how your brand reflects that. Ask your best clients what you've really solved for them, then build a powerful brand story that reflects your best results for future clients.

The answers might surprise you.

I used to say I'm a copywriter who writes websites and sales proposals. My clients told me I'm a confidence coach who helps them see their true value. Now I sell confidence, wrapped in copywriting, brand stories, and personalised sales training.

The faster you figure out what you really solve for people who truly value what you can do, the sooner you can niche down into your Ikigai service and write a better future for your brand.

As we learned selling millions of dollars of photos to 'no-photos-please' cruise guests on luxury ships, people don't buy things from people. They don't even buy the people behind the things we sell.

People only buy the way we make them feel, and the story we tell them to take them there.

This sense of authentic humility is what resonates with your dream clients, and brings them straight to your open door.

Sell with care!

ACKNOWLEDGEMENTS

So many people have helped me over the years that it would be impossible to acknowledge everybody. I've been lucky to have rubbed shoulders with good people and great mentors.

My dad, Don Dent, was the spark. He once gave me the best piece of business advice I've ever received, which was this: 'It doesn't matter which line of work you choose, as long as you always have a skill in yourself that you can rely on when things get tough.'

Off the back of that advice, I took a course in freelance journalism and travel writing, found my passion, and started a copywriting business alongside my former career in the travel industry. That advice not only saved my bacon, but also set me up for self-driven success that brings both money and joy into my life and work.

My brother, Rob Dent, has also shaped my success story. A long time ago, he believed in my skill, took a chance on me, and gave me the confidence to believe in myself.

To my mum, Jackie Dent, who taught me to love books and to hate split infinitives. Your unwavering ability to rise above has made me strong.

To my tribe of siblings with all your rhyming names – Ca, Sa, Ga, Rob, Wit, and Jay – and of course, Gemma, thanks for putting up with all my questions. I come from a long line of successful entrepreneurs, so your support means the world to me.

To Casey Bradford. Your insight into the world of psychology has had a profound impact. Thanks for letting me explore my ideas in a safe space.

To Sam Hudson, Sam Spence, and Mark Churcher, thanks for always being excited about my ambitious projects. If it weren't for the people like you in my life, nothing would ever get done.

To Murray and Elaine Simpson. I learned so much from both of you during my time in New Zealand. Your understanding of creating exceptional experiences for others has shaped my life's philosophy that we can change the way people feel just by changing their experience.

To Harriet Power, my editor. Thank you for asking all the right questions. This book has transformed significantly since its first draft, all because you had the insight to interrogate my ideas until they made sense. Your personal input has not only made this a better book, but has also made me a better brand storyteller.

To Kailey Salisbury, Marla Thompson, Mariana Coello, Harry Wallett, Samuel Boyce Miles, and the village who have made this book – thank you! It really does take a village!

For my advance reader team – who have been subjected to a book full of typos just to glean their valuable opinions – each of you has added immeasurable value to the final book.

To Derek Watson. Your quiet and often unseen mentorship continuously inspires me to look for the fun in life and work. Thanks for stepping in to make things better.

To my clients, good and bad! Collectively, you have taught me something immeasurable. You've shown me what I do best, which is to pull out what really matters and turn it into something worth having.

Finally, to you, the reader. If it weren't for readers like you who value the power of ideas, this book wouldn't exist. It's all here, because of you.

Recommended Reading

Many of the concepts explored in this book only touch on the depth of others, so I've put together my list of favourite reads that have somehow shaped my understanding of the world around me.

Each of these books can transform life and business for the better.

Daring Greatly by Brené Brown

This is a good read for combatting imposter syndrome. I've always felt that imposter syndrome is a healthy growth tool. It happens when we overestimate our own ability, then rise to meet the challenge. Daring Greatly reaffirms that, by highlighting how vulnerabilities in risk-taking lead to significant growth.

The Age of Empathy by Frans De Waal

Nature has always relied on building connections to thrive. Frans De Waal examines concepts like herd mentality and social bonds in animals, which translate seamlessly into building thriving communities in our human world. This is really useful if you want to grow your tribe.

Scientific Advertising by Claude C. Hopkins

Claude Hopkins was obsessed with understanding data in advertising. He measured, tracked, and tweaked his campaigns relentlessly until they worked perfectly. This short book consolidates his lessons in why people buy more easily in certain scenarios. His book is a century old and still rings true with today's best-kept marketing secrets.

Breakthrough Advertising by Eugene Schwartz

Eugene Schwartz is widely regarded as one of the most successful direct-response copywriters of all time. Like Claude Hopkins, he worked at a time which pre-dates modern technology and the digital era. His teachings are filled with human psychology. This book is a treasure trove of insightful techniques for driving mass demand with words and stories.

The Body Keeps the Score by Bessel van der Kolk

This book is primarily an exploration of how the mind and body are impacted by post-traumatic stress disorder. I've had PTSD for most of my adult life, and I've always felt that my personal experience living with hyperawareness has shaped my ability to craft powerful brand stories. The Body Keeps the Score has inspired my model of the reptile, the monkey, and the everyday jackass.

Start With Why by **Simon Sinek**

Inspiration comes from leadership, which starts with understanding why you want to lead. This short book is about building trust to inspire greatness in yourself and others.

Expert Secrets by Russell Brunson

Russell Brunson is one of the world's leading minds in e-commerce and online sales. Expert Secrets is about building customer loyalty through finding your business purpose, then monetising that purpose with stackable offers. This book is ideal if you want to build on your three offers that make money.

Creativity, Inc. by **Ed Catmull**

Humility is perfectly demonstrated in this gem of a book. Co-founder of Pixar Animation Studios, Ed Catmull has dedicated his life to understanding how to create an inspiring organisational culture. This book is the ultimate guide on active listening and true collaboration with the people you serve.

The Archetypes and the Collective Unconscious by **Carl Jung**

If you want to really get down into the nitty gritty of applied psychology, then Carl Jung's teachings on how our deep psychology shapes the way we behave is the ultimate read.

The Hero and the Outlaw by Margaret Mark and Carol S. Pearson

I've used this book as a textbook in my own business for years. It's a deep exploration of how archetypes shape powerful brands. If you're looking to delve deep into your preferred archetype, this is a brilliant supplementary read to Enriched Marketing

Illusions by Richard Bach

This is a short read that changed my life. It's one of those little books that likes to be gifted to others, and somehow always shows up at just the right time. I read it every few years, give it away, then magically seem to find another copy when it's most needed.

ABOUT THE AUTHOR

Natalie Dent is a professional sales copywriter and brand voice development consultant with over 20 years' experience in the sales and marketing arena.

Part South African, part English, part nomad, she's travelled the world in search of the human story.

Natalie's wealth of global cultural knowledge taps effortlessly into the nuances of sales psychology, while her experience in luxury tourism inspires meaningful customer journeys that are fundamentally about service before sales.

Natalie has written powerful sales campaigns for some of the world's most established brands.

She lives in Edinburgh with her pup, Puzzle.

ADDITIONAL RESOURCES

One of my greatest passions is helping people see and achieve their full potential. I like people to feel inspired, and I always look for ways to simplify complex ideas into human stories.

This book gives you the tools you need to empower your business with the perfect client, so you can make money doing something you love.

If you've found value here, there's a wealth of additional support on my website at enrichedmarketing.co.uk.

Resources range from free tools to personalised support and fully fledged services that take the work right off your plate. Take a look and see what suits you best.

If you've enjoyed reading my book, please do share the love and tell others about it too. If you're feeling ultra-generous today, please share your experience with a kind review wherever you feel most comfortable leaving one. You may also like to send me a message with your feedback via the website.

If you have any questions, you can always reach out to me by email at info@writtenbynatalie.co.uk

Thanks for reading my book. All that's left to do now is build the brand you love for the people you want to serve.

You've got this!

GET IN TOUCH

For all enquiries, including talks and appearances, please contact:

info@writtenbynatalie.co.uk
writtenbynatalie.co.uk
enrichedmarketing.co.uk

Follow Me: @copywriternatalie
Connect on Linkedin: linkedin.com/in/copywriternatalie

If you have any questions, would like to explore your ideas, or just want to share your opinion, please don't be shy!

I would love to hear from you.

Best,

Natalie